How to RAISE A PARENT

Becoming a Conscious Parent in an Unconscious World

ELLEN F. GOTTLIEB

Copyright © 2021 by Ellen F. Gottlieb, Founder of Enlightened Parenting

All rights reserved.

Published by Red Penguin Books

Bellerose Village, New York

Library of Congress Control Number: 2021907911

ISBN

Print 978-1-63777-033-7/978-1-63777-087-0

Digital 978-1-63777-033-7

Edited By: David R. Ord

Illustrated By: Megan Mack

No part of this book may be reproduced in any form or by any electronic or mechanical means, including information storage and retrieval systems, without written permission from the author, except for the use of brief quotations in a book review.

This book is dedicated to my loving husband, Sam, and to my precious daughters, Deena and Sara. You are my greatest teachers. You mean the world to me and the depth of my love for each of you is infinite. You have my heart.

This book is also dedicated to the memory of my sister, Robin Hope, who always showed enormous courage, strength, grace, and resilience in the face of extraordinary challenges and suffering, and who taught me the true meaning of unconditional love and acceptance of the as is.

CONTENTS

A Special Note from Dr. Shefali	ix
Testimonials	xi
Introduction	xv

PART 1
BUILDING CONNECTIONS

1. NON-REACTIVITY	3
Computer Glitches	8
Connection, Not Correction	10
Don't Take The Bait	13
What Goes Around Comes Around	15
A Hair-Raising Situation	17
2. EMOTIONAL TOLERANCE	23
Taming the Green-Eyed Monster	29
An Invitation to Joy	34
Don't Be a Hijacker	37
3. PROCESS VERSUS OUTCOME	41
Thumbs Up	43
Making the Grade	45
Raising a Child, Not a Resume	48
A Swing and a Miss	50

PART 2
CREATING BOUNDARIES: IMPARTING SAFETY THROUGH LIMITS AND CONNECTION

4. ESSENTIAL BOUNDARIES	61
Line in the Sand	63
On-Call	64
Prize and Punishment	66
Begging for Boundaries	70

5. BREACHING ESSENTIAL BOUNDARIES - CHEATING, STEALING, AND LYING	75
And I'll Lie If I Want To…	76
…But I Don't Need To	80
Sticky Fingers	82
Rated "C" for Conscious	84
6. NON-ESSENTIAL BOUNDARIES	87
Candy Land	88
Swimming Upstream	90
7. CONSEQUENCES VERSUS PUNISHMENTS	95
Tug-of-War	96
It's All Downhill	99
8. WHEN ONE PARENT JUST DOESN'T GET IT!	103
Critical Coaching	105
9. THE TERRIFYING TEENAGE YEARS	113
Break a Leg	114
Cut from a Different Cloth	117
Inside Out	120

PART 3

THE 11TH COMMANDMENT - HONOR THY CHILD

10. CHILDREN ARE OUR MIRRORS	129
A Weighty Issue	132
Mirror, Mirror	137
11. SELF-COMPASSION	141
Girl Power	142
It's Never Too Late…	144
12. RESILIENCE	149
Pain Is Gain	152
13. DETACHMENT	155
The Art of Letting Go	157
Applying Consciousness	159

14. DISCERN AND ATTUNE	163
Stage Fright	164
To Err is Human, to Apologize Is Mindful	169
Family Values	171
15. AUTHENTICITY AND ABUNDANCE	175
An Anxious Legacy	177
16. OPTIONS: ACCEPT, LEAVE, OR CHANGE	183
The Art of Acceptance	184
17. POWER AND RESPONSIBILITY	189
Acceptance Breeds Success	191
18. EMOTIONAL FREEDOM THROUGH CONSCIOUS LIVING	195

PART 4
THE CONSCIOUS TOOLBOX

THE CONSCIOUS TOOLBOX	201
Role Play	201
Distraction	203
Nurture Nature	205
Offer Options	206
Autonomy Rocks	207
Turn Criticism to Compliments	210
Avoid Labels	211
Set the Conditions	212
Get Buy-In	213
Sibling Rivalry	216
Special Time	217
Family Meetings	219
Teachable Moments: Listening Without Lecturing	220
Use Direct-Examination, not Cross-Examination	221
Honesty is the Best Policy	223
Powerful Phrases	224
Say This Instead of That	225
Promote Opportunities for Service	226
Promote Opportunities for Self-Expression	227
Practice Self-Care, Meditation, and Self-Compassion	228

Keep a Journal	230
Inculcate Gratitude	231
Send Your Child a Note to Thank Them for Raising You	233
Final Thoughts	237
Acknowledgments	241
About the Author	245

A SPECIAL NOTE FROM DR. SHEFALI

Conscious parenting helps raise us parents into growth and healing. By doing this, our children thrive. Ellen's wonderful book paves the way for parents to apply its principles in a grounded, concrete, and practical way. These words will encourage you to build a stronger connection with your kids and help them discover their authentic selves.

It's a must-read for every parent who wishes to heal and fortify their relationship with their children. Your children will thank you for this.

Dr. Shefali Tsabary

New York Times best-selling author of *The Conscious Parent* and *The Awakened Family*

TESTIMONIALS

Ellen has been an awesome spiritual guide and teacher for me. My work with her has changed the trajectory of my life and I am so grateful as I have learned so many invaluable lessons. Now I know how to live a more mindful, joyful life, grounded in humility, self-responsibility, and gratitude. I have also learned to stay firmly rooted in the present moment without regard to outcomes. I know I will be a better parent someday because of the teachings of her book.

~ Jared W., Equity/Derivatives/Options Trader, Millennial

I am so grateful to have Ellen in my life. Because of our work together, I am a better businessperson, a better leader, a better husband, and most importantly a better dad. She has served as a steady hand of guidance which has helped me much more than I can ever explain.

Her ability to communicate and write is extremely helpful. Her ability to connect with people on the truth that guides them is special. Her ability to challenge one's core in a way that helps them develop and grow is amazing. Her ability to teach on a subject that is so important, yet difficult, is God-

given. But what makes her preeminent is her selfless service to others which is the purpose of her extraordinary book.

Her wisdom has been life-changing for me. Because of her efforts, I have never been happier. She is the origin of my progress and self-awareness.

~ Jimmy S., CEO, Business Leader, Entrepreneur, father of two

---

I am so thankful to Ellen for the important lessons that she has taught me. She gently guided and supported me through this process of conscious parenting. As a result, I have learned to live and parent our twin daughters more mindfully!

~ Jennifer L., Assistant Principal, mother of two

Despite serious family issues and the crisis of the pandemic of 2020, this has been the best year of my life and I have Ellen to thank.

~ James K., Business Manager, Restaurateur, Sports Podcaster

Ellen's simple yet deeply introspective work has given me skills and power I never knew I had.

~ David A., Professional Athlete, Entrepreneur, father of two

---

Ellen is amazing! I am so grateful to her as she has helped me and my family enormously. Her book will help every parent connect better with their children.

~ Len L., Head of Physical Plant Operations, father of two

I feel so much lighter having worked with Ellen. Our time together always feels very nourishing and offers a sense of confidence and relief.

~ Pippa L., Creative Director, Brand Advisor, Consultant, mother of two

---

I am so grateful for all of Ellen's help, guidance, and love. Ellen is my mentor, sister, friend, and teacher, and she has given me so much hope for a joy-filled life. Mindful parenting is a whole new paradigm, and Ellen knows how to teach it so well.

~ Tajinder K., Engineer, mother of two

I am grateful to Ellen for really hearing me. Her help and support guide me to learn to be more trusting and joyful in all of my roles, especially that of mother. I can see that there are many more days of fun and joy ahead.

~ Shira P., Director of Development; Non-Profit Fundraiser, mother of two

---

We met Ellen through our son's therapist and working with her has improved our family dynamics. She taught us some basic methods and they really worked. She is both understanding as well as caring. Wish we had met her years ago, but better late than never.

~ David & Gloria C., Retired Educator and Administrator, parents of two adults

I am so grateful to Ellen! Thanks to her my relationship with my daughter and my two sons is so much better than it used to be. I've become more loving, kind, and understanding. Ellen has taught me how to listen before reacting. She has helped me to appreciate the fact that all my children have feelings, thoughts, and creativity that I had never seen or noticed before. She is simply the best and I cannot thank her enough for all she has done for me and my family. I am forever grateful to her.

~ Maureen V., Police Officer, Entrepreneur, mother of three

I am so grateful to Ellen for guiding me on this journey of conscious parenting! I wish I had learned 21 years ago what I learned now. Connection is everything and providing for my child's physical necessities is not enough. Thank you, Ellen, for opening my eyes to these essential parts of parenting.

~ Risa B., Graphic Designer, Artist, mother of three

Now that I have learned about mindful parenting with Ellen, I feel like I have a superpower and it feels fantastic. I would never have imagined that parenting could be this joyful.

~ Joel. P., College Professor

INTRODUCTION

What You Will Learn By Reading This Book

All caregivers and parents - whether biological, adoptive, foster or surrogate - need to raise themselves as they raise their child. The parent who finds their own voice and who understands their own emotional matrix is in the best position to raise an emotionally healthy child. The child of that parent is the one more likely to make better decisions in adolescence and thereafter, the one who is more likely to experience a better trajectory in life and soar, and the one who will be less enslaved by the confines of generational suffering. All too often parents clip their child's wings and then demand that they fly. This book will teach parents how to avoid the pitfalls and perils of parenting unconsciously.

Becoming more awakened to one's own spiritual wants and needs will also favorably impact all relationships as one learns to create deeper and more meaningful connections and boundaries with parents, partners, and friends. That is the beauty of this work and the goal of this book.

This book is a guide for raising yourself and your child at the same time. Parenting mindfully is sacred work, as it is through this vehicle that parents can hope to not only raise but to elevate their children to live their most joyful and satisfying lives. The work of mindful parenting spans race, religion, ethnicity, nationality, gender, along with sexual orientation and identification.

The manner in which a child is raised is ordinarily a reflection of the way that their parents were raised. Often, looking at the parents' nature will determine whether the child's quest will be unending or fulfilled. This is why the work of conscious parenting requires the parent to raise themselves first. Then the parents can teach their children that they are worthy and good enough in their parents' eyes.

These ideas are intended to help parents become more mindful so that their families can transition from dysfunction to function, from chaos to tranquility, from emotional unsteadiness to stability, and from suffering to joy. There is no more important relationship in life than that of parent and child. It is by honoring that relationship in the most meaningful ways that both parents and their children can grow and thrive.

The keys are in every parent's hands. Join me in unlocking the door by opening your soul to the most important work on the planet. This is the path to freedom, power, and joy, and it is a remarkable journey.

How to Raise Emotional Intelligence

Strong emotional intelligence provides the foundation for a spiritual, healthy, and peaceful life. It is a true societal injustice that this essential pillar of life is largely ignored by the educational system. Even more troubling is that the most well-intentioned parents barely have a rudimentary understanding of their own emotional template. Therefore, instead of elevating their children to live their best lives, sadly, parents inadvertently pass on the legacy of their own emotional baggage filled with suffering, stress, misery, drama, and trauma from generation to generation.

When a child is imbued with an understanding of their internal emotional life, and is taught how to cope in the world, they will gain self-confidence, humility, empathy, and gratitude. The child who learns to live comfortably in their own skin is one whose life's trajectory is unlimited. This is the blueprint for a joyful life. While societal norms are often governed by the illusion that perfect scores, elite colleges, and prestigious careers provide the most likely path to success and happiness, the truth is that inner awareness and comfort are the real keys.

How to Raise a Parent

The antidote to the legacy of emotional toxicity is conscious parenting through conscious living. A conscious parent is one who has disentangled and awoken from their own emotional matrix, detached from ordinary thoughts, fears, and desires. They have become connected to their own needs and aspirations, and have learned to practice self-care in order to be able to give freely and neutrally to their children without the burden of their own egoic desires. They have raised their emotional intelligence so that they in turn can raise a confident, humble child who has a strong sense of self.

So, how do you do it? Not unlike exercising to build stronger muscles, emotional intelligence is developed by repeatedly exercising the muscle of mindfulness. This requires parents to be willing to continuously assess their own patterns, habits, thoughts, responses, and reactions. As they do this, they build the inner awareness necessary to create healthy connections with their children. It is akin to cleaning up one's emotional landscape. This will ultimately allow parents to create more authentic and healthy relationships with their children. This process requires patience, practice, courage, and love.

As with the ocean, where one can only see above the surface, the words stated by a parent reflect only the surface of their feelings. Beneath those words lies an enormous expanse of thoughts and feelings expressed by the parent through non-verbal communication and cues. Children pick up less from their parents' words than from their energy, tone, and body language.

Unfortunately, many parents remain blind to the damage they are subtly causing with an offhand comment or a seemingly casual gesture. Their subconscious is deeply entrenched in intergenerational patterns of behavior, expectations, feelings, and judgments of themselves and of the world. If a parent chooses to awaken, they must be willing to dive in and examine their thoughts, feelings, and behaviors which lurk beneath the surface. A parent who is willing to do this challenging inner work inevitably releases the next generation from becoming stuck in those murky waters.

While the child hears a parent's words, the parent must always be mindful of the fact that the child is picking up on the unspoken but ever-present messages. The parent's words may inform the child of whether the water is calm or fierce. However, what lies beneath the surface offers the greatest clues as to the depth and current of the parent's true feelings. Essentially, this means that a parent must understand that not only are their words experienced by their child, but also their intonations, their energy, their mood, and perhaps their unspoken yet powerful messages about family dynamics.

For all of these reasons, in order to become a conscious parent, one must become aware of the thoughts and feelings that take them away from being present and from responding in the moment. Conscious living allows a person to engage with life with the understanding that they are co-creating each life experience as it unfolds. The inverse belief, that life happens to them, can result in feelings of anger, disempowerment, fear, anxiety, and victimhood.

Once it is understood that the endless chatter in one's mind is impermanent and merely the result of habitual patterns, the window opens to allow for change. It all begins in the present moment with a willingness and openness to new ideas of impermanence and exploration. It also requires patience and practice to forgo long-held and deeply entrenched patterns of thoughts, behaviors, and reactions.

When a parent is ready to embrace new ways of being, and in turn new ways of parenting, they can recognize their deep conditioning. Instead of getting stuck on thoughts, imagine the idea of a "train of thought." As quickly as a thought arrives, it can be placed on that proverbial train and released. Thoughts that have been ingrained in one's mind from an early age tend to be repeated incessantly throughout life. The work of mindfulness is to learn to detach from repetitive thoughts so that they can be seen as the illusions they are. This is the path to true freedom and joy.

Each chapter is highlighted by examples that demonstrate the ideas and lessons presented. Since stories allow people to store memories, I hope that these vignettes will resonate with you and provide insight and guidance about these fundamental principles. These stories are not attributable to any particular person or family, including my own. Feminine or masculine pronouns are used interchangeably since these concepts are applicable to all parents and children.

PART 1
BUILDING CONNECTIONS

There are two fundamental questions to which each living human being seeks answers throughout life:

Do you hear me?
Am I worthy?

Parents' actions constantly inform a child's answers to these questions about themselves. When a parent has learned to set aside their own ego and be more aware as they encounter their child, that child is likely to have greater self-worth. This is the child who is more likely to find their voice and thrive in the world. On the other hand, where a parent's actions are mindless, this is the child who is more likely to have a lifelong unquenchable thirst for approval, never feeling worthy and secure.

When the child feels that their voice matters and that their essence is honored exactly as it is, the answers to those two fundamental questions flow naturally. This is the child who will feel worthy and valued, and this is the child who will feel free to navigate the world more easily. Unconditional acceptance of a child is essential to mindful parenting. It leads to an internal sense of value and worth that only the child needs to define and understand. Other people's judgment of them will become irrelevant.

This book offers pragmatic, fundamental tools that can be used as a parent encounters their child on a moment-to-moment basis. It addresses the basic and fundamental tenets of mindful parenting: ***connection*** and ***boundaries***. Connection as a concept defines what it means to be mindful, focused in the present moment, and detached from one's ego. It is through deep and trusting connection that the parent-child bond will thrive. True connection, premised on unconditional love, is essential for the child to feel validated and worthy, and to know that they are heard.

There are many ways to manifest profound connection with a child and they begin with non-reactivity. Once deep, unconditional connection has been established between the parent and child, that relationship can develop and flow naturally as the child will trust that they will not be admonished regardless of their behavior.

1 NON-REACTIVITY

- Will yelling change the outcome?
- Will unleashing anger teach a lesson or embed fear?
- Whose need is being served by yelling - the child's or the parent's?
- Does my child's developmental age play a role in the behavior I am witnessing?
- Am I willing to apologize to my child for my mindless reaction?
- Can I delay my need for immediate release of my feelings so that I can enjoy the later satisfaction of having exercised restraint and therefore not having wounded my child?

Parents often feel the temptation to nag and yell at their children, unleashing their anger and frustration. This is often done under the guise of teaching. **Little do parents realize that when they yell, blame, shame, and criticize their child, they are actually wounding them.**

Parents feel that they have free rein to let loose on their children if their child makes a mistake, exercises bad judgment, behaves poorly, or breaches an essential boundary. This desire to yell is perceived as an entitlement attached to the parent's authority. Often this was done to the parents themselves by their parents, which affords them implicit permission to do it to their children. Parents seem to conveniently forget that they despised this same behavior when they were children.

The true path to mindful parenting is the recognition that the parent-child relationship is not a hierarchy, but a partnership. The parent should guide the child and allow the child's essence to unfold, but the parent is not an omnipotent dictator. Seen from this point of view, parents can begin to recognize the importance of controlling their own reactions rather than their child's behavior.

Because of the unspoken but powerful illusion that the parent has ultimate control, and that they can and should exert their control over their child, inherent in the parent's sense of entitlement is the right to yell at their child even at the slightest infraction. It is critical to remember that the family home is not chosen by the child. Rather, children are hostages in their homes. This obligates parents to treat their children with the utmost care and respect. While children may have two homes or may occasionally sleep at the home of a relative or friend, they cannot join another family or select other parents.

Therefore, whether your child experiences their home as a prison or a sanctuary will make all the difference in their self-perception, and ultimately in their life's trajectory. This is why the way a child is consistently treated by their parents will provide the answers to these fundamental questions:

Do you hear me? Am I worthy?

Coffee Break-Down

Chloe, a senior account executive, has been preparing for months to pitch a new and potentially very profitable client. Closing this deal is important to the future of her career, and a major bonus and promotion depend on sealing it. The morning of the meeting she was excitedly showing her best friend the colorful materials she printed.

Her friend accidentally spilled a full cup of coffee all over Chloe's documents and started frantically trying to clean up the mess. There was not enough time before the meeting to reprint all the materials. Chloe was angst-ridden, but she was intuitively understanding despite her frustration and upset. She reminded her friend that it was an accident, that the client will still be able to read the relevant materials, and that she still has a few minutes to reprint the most important pages.

Now imagine this same scenario, except that Chloe is sitting alone at her kitchen table enjoying her morning coffee and making final preparations for the meeting. Her six-year-old son Joe, dressed in his favorite superhero costume, was feeling his mother's contagious, exuberant energy. He was joyfully running around the kitchen table waving his favorite plastic sword which inadvertently knocked over that same cup of coffee and damaged her materials. Chloe went into a rage. She screamed, yelled, and reprimanded Joe for running around the kitchen table waving his sword, even though she was fully cognizant of the fun he was having just a few moments earlier.

When Chloe's friend damaged her important materials, she was able to flow with the moment without an outward reaction while she also created effective solutions. When her son Joe was the inadvertent culprit, she was unable to control her reaction and she yelled at him.

This type of scenario plays out all the time. A parent is more likely to protect a friend because they deeply appreciate that connection and do not want to damage, strain, or lose it. Under identical circumstances, the same parent feels free to unleash their fury onto their child because they inherently understand that their child cannot leave, as they are totally dependent on them. Friends can leave, whereas children cannot.

Why do parents feel free to disregard the feelings of their children without hesitation, while being more sensitive to the feelings and needs of their friends? While parents should not treat their children as though they are their friends, they should treat their children at least as well as they treat their friends. But frankly, aren't children owed even more than this? Shouldn't they be treated with the utmost respect?

A child's emotional evolution depends on their parent's careful and mindful responses to them at each of their developmental stages and ages. Their home should be a safe haven rather than a prison. Before unleashing a mindless reaction onto their child, a wise parent will ask themselves whether they want to have a mess to clean up. In other words, in the aftermath of an outburst, the parent has to mend hurt feelings. On the other hand, it is extremely gratifying to have paused and refrained from reacting, recognizing that they did not inflict yet another emotional wound.

Since Joe was only six years old, it was incumbent upon Chloe to recognize that he was playfully enjoying his mother's company. Just as her friend had no ill intent, neither did Joe. His developmental age did not allow him to consider the future consequences of his actions.

Chloe, being a mindful mother, realized immediately that she had been unfair to react as she did and that she needed to apologize. She understood the importance of expressing remorse for her outburst, seeing it as a way to teach Joe that his feelings matter and that there is power in accepting responsibility for her error.

The parent who pauses and breathes before unleashing their uncontrolled emotions onto their child is a parent who is awakened. While a parent often feels entitled to react to a child's untoward behavior, the parent who waits just a few moments instead of reacting instantly to an infraction will ultimately feel empowered. The simple act of pausing before reacting will often allow the parent the moment needed to choose to withhold a harsh reaction realizing that in doing so, they will not belittle their child. This avoids inflicting an invisible yet deep emotional wound onto their child.

When a child is yelled at by a parent for an infraction, the child does not love the parent less. Instead, they turn their parent's obvious disappointment, disapproval, and unhappiness inward and they love themselves less. Over time, this creates internal disharmony and crushes the child's self-esteem and spirit.

People often ask whether their children will learn critical life lessons if parents choose not to express their anger in response to "bad" behavior. Rest assured, they will. Children will learn essential lessons and exhibit more acceptable behavior when they are not blamed, criticized, or shamed. The opportunity for the child to learn and to shift their behavior exists in the space where the parent does not react, but instead remains calm and neutral.

A parent's reaction can engender fear and anger in their child. **Every time a parent unleashes anger onto their child, they are unwittingly scarring that child's soul.** Whether the child failed a test, forgot to walk the dog, lost the new sweater, or accidentally filled the car with diesel fuel, yelling will not alter the outcome. The test will still be failed, the dog still not walked, the sweater still lost, and the engine still ruined.

A child who has been belittled repeatedly by a parent will have less self-confidence and more anxiety. Whether they are admonished for minor infractions, shamed for differences of opinion, criticized for their judgment, or screamed at for larger offenses, the parent's reaction will have a lasting impact while not changing their child's long-term behavior. Children do not learn by being yelled at, nagged, criticized, shamed, or blamed.

Most parents know never to hit or spank their children since this can cause physical injury. The scars and bruises become obvious, and caring parents do not intend to do harm. Sadly, often those same parents feel free to inflict reactive and mindless verbal outbursts onto their children causing deep and permanent, albeit invisible, injury to the child's spirit and soul.

Computer Glitches

> *Before laptop computers were standard in most homes, the parents of ten-year-old Lucy purchased a single expensive laptop for shared family use. Shortly thereafter, Lucy's father Ricky sat down to use it and found that it wasn't functioning properly. Needless to say, he was frustrated.*

> *When Lucy saw her father's confusion, irritation, and anger, she tearfully explained, with her piggy-bank in hand, that several days earlier she had spilled an entire glass of water onto the keyboard. She had been in a panic since it happened. When the damage became apparent to her father, she confessed with terror in her eyes.*

Ricky and his wife Ethel each took a breath, and at first considered that perhaps the computer could be fixed. Only after learning it was destroyed, was Ricky tempted to shout at Lucy. Instead, they convened a family meeting to discuss rules about computer use. When asked, each family member acknowledged that they often ate and drank while using the computer.

Instead of yelling, Ricky and Ethel thanked Lucy for teaching the family a very important lesson - that computers are fragile. They created a new rule that food and drink were not to be consumed while using electronic devices. Lucy was relieved. Although the computer was ruined, Lucy's self-esteem remained intact.

This mindful response to a frustrating event did not result in Lucy carelessly damaging other devices. Rather, it caused her to be much more careful in the future. Yelling does not serve children. Instead, it wounds them. While the situation was handled in a mindful manner, Ricky decided that although it was an accident and Lucy was not reprimanded or punished, there were more lessons to be learned from this experience.

Since actions have natural consequences, at that family meeting everyone was informed that sadly the computer would not be replaced immediately. Everyone in the family felt the pain of not having internet access for a while. After several months of savings with contributions by each family member, a new computer was finally purchased.

In those intervening months before the purchase of a new computer, there was neither any discussion about the old computer nor any complaining about not having a computer to use. When a new computer was finally purchased, Lucy thoroughly enjoyed pointing out the irony of finding Ricky enjoying a full cup of soda while using it only a day after it was purchased. She gently reminded him that perhaps that was unwise and they both giggled. This lesson taught Lucy not only to be careful while using devices, but also that she remains worthy even when she makes a costly error.

Non-reactivity is important when larger issues occur like the story of the broken computer, as mindfulness must be applied consistently and regularly. A child's sense of self is damaged by the parent who explodes even occasionally, as well as by the parent who regularly nags and expresses constant disappointment.

Connection, Not Correction

> *Nancy, a single mother and successful physician, was frustrated that her eight- and nine-year-old children had become inured to her yelling and were perpetually uncooperative in doing even the most basic tasks. They refused to do their homework, help with chores, brush their teeth, or wake up on time for school. Tired of nagging and yelling, she was at her wit's end. She had tried both punishments and rewards, and neither was effective. She wanted to "fix her kids."*

Instead of focusing on her children, Nancy needed to shift her own behavior and responses to her children. At first, she was guarded and frustrated as she could not fathom what she could possibly have been doing wrong. She soon started to realize that due to her constant nagging, the energy in her home was miserable. There was no joy in anyone's life.

Desperate to blame her children, she protested that no one could have any fun when the kids were so uncooperative and obnoxious. Everyone in the family was exasperated. This overwhelmed mother had no idea that her energy, demands, and frustration were creating disharmony, and that her children's emotional needs were being entirely unmet.

> ***When a child behaves in a way that the parent finds inappropriate, untoward, or intolerable, there is an unmet need beneath the behavior that must be discerned.*** *Figuring out what that need is and attempting to meet it is the work of the conscious parent. Mindful parenting is often akin to detective work. For this family, it was time to break conditioned, habituated patterns. Doing so always begins with the parent.*

In order for Nancy to stop her knee-jerk reactions to her kids, she needed to take care of her own needs first. Self-care lays the groundwork for conscious parenting, as the parent can open space within themselves to be more patient and consistent in their interactions with their children. A re-energized parent is a gift to their children.

With the help of her mindful parenting coach, Nancy realized that her home was not functioning well. It felt to her as though each family member was living on a different planet. Her children had shut down and consequently had shut her out. Their lack of cooperation was their way of silently screaming at her to change her ways so she could begin to meet their physical and emotional needs. She began to understand that based on their ages and developmental stages, her agenda was unreasonable and unattainable, especially when she persistently expressed it through anger and criticism.

Nancy needed to cede control of her agenda and give her children her undivided attention in a joyful way. Through their challenging behavior, her children were begging her to wake up and thus were offering her a great gift in the form of a lesson that she needed to be unconditionally present and engaged with them. **A mindful parent needs to cede control in order to seed joy!**

It was time for a huge shift in Nancy's behavior and expectations. Rather than experiencing their mom's impatience, frustration, nagging, disappointment, and yelling, it was time for them to experience her in a new way. This meant that initially, she had to let go of her need for a perfectly-run home. At first, she would have to allow takeout for dinner, unmade beds, unfinished homework, and later bedtimes. She had to rebuild trust, which in turn would rebuild cooperation.

As to basic essential tasks, such as showering and brushing teeth, she needed to cajole the children in a new way by making those activities pleasant and even fun. They could all brush their teeth together and have a contest to see who could blow the biggest bubble while giggling without worrying about the mess on the floor. She told them that after showers, there would be evening snacks and bedtime stories. **The path to repairing these relationships was found through connection and communication rather than through control and correction.**

Nancy's children needed to trust that there would be no screaming, pestering, or punishment. Instead, they could expect unconditional love and connection. They needed to be seen and heard by their mother in a new light, devoid of her desire for control of their physical environment. It was time to course-correct without lamenting the past.

Within just a few days of Nancy's shifts in her behavior, her children began cooperating. They were more excited to come home from school and tell her about their days. They were willing to help more with chores and get basic things done, as that resulted in more time with their mother. Nancy learned the critical lesson that she neither could, nor should try to fix her children as they are wonderful just as they are.

Children are flexible and willing to shift their behavior once they are truly convinced that they can trust their parents to shift their responses and to accept them unconditionally. Initially, children may not trust that their parent's behavior has truly changed so they may raise the stakes on their own untoward behaviors. Children tend to up the ante to test whether things have really changed. This is to be expected and handled with equanimity and patience.

With time, patience, and consistency, children will begin to trust this new paradigm and in turn they will be more cooperative. **Cooperation is enhanced through love and connection, which every child craves, rather than through correction and control which actually cause untoward behaviors to persist.** Also, those children whose parents do not regularly react mindlessly, routinely withholding shame, blame, and scolding, will find that their children can tolerate when unpleasant things happen to them because they have greater self-esteem.

Don't Take The Bait

> *A group of four 4th-grade girlfriends were sitting at a cluster of desks working on individual art projects when one of them, Haley, was handed a note signed by the others which said, "We hate you. You stink. We no longer want to be friends with you." Upon reading the note, Haley ripped it into shreds, slowly dropping each piece into the garbage pail. She then returned to her desk and continued working silently on her art project. The other girls, perplexed at her lack of reaction, watched silently. They had expected a dramatic and distraught reaction from Haley.*

When Haley returned home, she expressed her sadness to her parents who helped her process her feelings as her tears flowed. Her emotional reaction was handled privately without any outside intervention or drama.

Since Haley's parents understood that sometimes young girls will do these things to one another, they did not contact the school or the teacher. Most importantly, they taught Haley that the other girls were responsible for their own behavior. She need not see herself as a victim, and she mindfully refused to give those other girls the satisfaction of creating any drama and getting any attention they craved.

Normally this type of ugly, bullying behavior would cause tremendous drama in a classroom and beyond. Often, the faculty would intervene, the parents of the aggrieved student would demand action, and there would be an intense reaction all around.

Such agitation was avoided because Haley's parents had taught her the essence of mindfulness, which in turn deprived the other girls of their anticipated response. They too learned a valuable lesson about how to feel empowered. They watched their ex-friend handle this situation with grace and strength. Haley knew that this ugly behavior had little to do with her. This was their story, not hers.

What Goes Around Comes Around

Rosie was cyber-bullied in 5th-grade. Three boys created a website about her, depicting her in horrid, profane ways. Her parents were furious and wanted justice. They wanted the parents of those boys to pay for their sons' stupid, ugly behavior. Because her parents felt so aggrieved for their daughter, whom they saw as a victim, they in turn, wanted the other families to suffer. Rosie's father, an attorney, wanted to file a lawsuit against those parents and the school district. This occurred in the early days of cyber-bullying and no one, including the school district, knew how to handle it.

Thanks to many lessons in mindfulness, Rosie wisely asked her parents not to intervene. She understood that this nasty behavior reflected on those boys, not on her. She had learned early on that she was not responsible for and could not control the behavior of others.

While she was sad and embarrassed about this incident, she sensed that those boys would have a more difficult time handling what they had done to her as time passed. She chose not to see herself as a victim, but merely as a player in their drama, albeit an incidental and involuntary one. She taught her parents a great lesson in non-reactivity.

Teaching a child to breathe for a few seconds when a feeling of anger wells up within them, rather than to react instantly, is a critical lesson in equanimity. Children learn to use their breath when parents model this behavior. This helps to control the instinct to mimic the ugly behavior that triggered the reaction in the first place. In fact, as Rosie taught by example, withholding one's reaction is a show of strength, while the feelings associated with the event can and should be handled and processed privately.

It is essential for parents to teach their children the lesson that no one can control anyone else's behaviors or feelings. When a person is strong and secure internally, no one can affect how they feel about themselves. To this day, more than ten years later, when Rosie happens to see one of those boys, they are too embarrassed to look at her. She has chosen not to create a worldview of herself as a victim. The bullies in this drama have become the victims. She, the intended victim, is the victor.

A Hair-Raising Situation

Maria, a sixteen-year-old, had a haircut that ended up being way too short. She felt she looked like a little boy and hated it. Both Maria and her mother were upset, especially because it was prom night. Maria even considered not going to prom because she was so embarrassed. Her mother humorously inquired as to whether she intended to remain hidden at home for the next few months.

Since Maria's hair would take time to grow back, her mother did not want to upset her daughter any more than she was already. Instead, she empathized with Maria's feelings. While her mother was tempted to try to protect Maria by telling her that her new hairstyle looked stunning and sophisticated, she wisely refrained from doing so, as Maria would have known that her mother was placating her. This would have dismissed the reality of the situation and invalidated Maria's feelings.

Instead, she allowed Maria to express her misery about the haircut while she neutralized her own feelings. She reminisced with her daughter about the time when she had colored her hair bright pink during high school for a school play and was terribly embarrassed and upset. Ultimately, Maria got dressed up that evening, put on earrings and makeup, and went to prom.

Non-reaction inevitably requires the parent to choose connection rather than criticism and correction. **The three keys to mindful parenting are *connection, connection, connection.***

Once a child trusts that they are deeply loved and unconditionally accepted without judgment, they can connect to their true essence and find their authentic voice. Children can often sense when their parents are lying although they may not know quite how to label it. This is why it is crucial that parents are authentic when they respond to their children. To do so, they must first do the hard work of clearing up their own emotional landscape.

Parents often mistakenly believe that their children will thrive only if they have the right pedigree, extra-curricular activities, social connections, looks, and education. While those factors are not unimportant, they are secondary to an internal sense of well-being and worthiness. Each child primarily needs to have their emotional needs met by a parent who listens without reaction as the child navigates their way.

A child's inner sense of self is one of the most important factors in determining whether they are likely to soar or sink. The child who feels whole and worthy, with humility and gratitude, will more likely be directed toward their true passions in life. This is the child who will invite, manifest, and attract the energy needed to reach and exceed their goals.

When a parent is feeling triggered by their child, the parent should pause and consider these questions before speaking:

- Am I reacting or responding to my child?
- Am I feeling angry and in lack, or am I able to stay neutral and in abundance?
- Are my thoughts focused in the past (in regret) or in the future (in worry), or are they firmly grounded in the present moment?
- Am I afraid? If so, what is causing my fear?
- Can I remain at peace regardless of what is happening?
- Do I have expectations that have not been fulfilled? If so, what are they, and are they valid?
- Can I release those expectations and accept this present moment as it is?
- Can I accept that this trigger is due to something within me, and is not related to my child's behavior?
- Am I focused on the process and the lessons to be learned rather than the outcome?
- What feelings are beneath my panic and worry?
- What are my unmet needs at this moment?
- Can I be silent and sit with my uncomfortable feelings calmly until they dissipate?
- Can I ride this emotional wave without involving my child in it?

- Can I self-soothe so that in turn I can be present for my child?
- Can I remain in a state of flow regardless of what is happening externally?

Connection is the essential cornerstone to the development of self-control and self-confidence in children. Parents are the guiding forces in their child's life and with unconditional connection, the child's authentic sense of self can blossom and flourish.

NOTES

2 EMOTIONAL TOLERANCE

- **Do I feel overwhelmed by my child's "negative" emotions?**
- **Am I afraid to allow my child to feel their feelings fully?**
- **What will happen if my child is sad, angry, or jealous?**
- **Are these feelings temporary?**
- **Will they have long-lasting effects?**
- **How do I feel when I cannot fix or change the way my child feels?**

I often hear parents say that they are only as happy as their least happy child. But is it true that parents can only feel joyful if their children are happy? Is it true that children should feel happy all the time?

I suggest that these are pervasive illusions that cause inordinate stress and sadness among parents and their children. To the contrary, emotional intelligence implies that it is a mistake to make happiness the goal, since happiness is elusive and temporary.

Despite the stated principle enunciated by our founding parents in the United States Declaration of Independence, that the pursuit of happiness is an inalienable right, to actually pursue happiness is to court disaster. Rather, parents and children must learn that the entire spectrum of emotions needs to be accepted and tolerated without resistance.

When parents are asked if they have ever experienced an emotion other than happiness, naturally every adult responds that they have. Why then do parents insist that their children must always feel happy? Why is that single feeling the only acceptable one? Perhaps it is because most adults have not learned to tolerate the breadth of their own feelings, so in turn, they cannot tolerate that of their children.

Learning to tolerate the full spectrum of their own and their children's feelings is counterintuitive to most people. However, learning this skill is the path to emotional literacy and inevitably reduces suffering. Acceptance of whatever is happening in the present moment is liberating, empowering, and ultimately joyful.

Becoming comfortable with uncomfortable feelings is one of the keys to living a conscious life. In doing so, feelings are no longer labeled as "good" (e.g. happy) or "bad" (e.g. sad, angry, frustrated, jealous), or as "positive" or "negative." Such mindless dualism is an illusion which creates suffering.

In seeking to protect their children from emotions which are conventionally labeled as negative, parents often create checklists, agendas, and goals that their children must reach in order to achieve happiness. This is a trap that inevitably creates the very unhappiness that parents seek and hope to avoid. It is empowering for children to learn that all feelings can be experienced without judgment, that they are temporary, and that they will be metabolized and diffused at just the right time regardless of how long that might take.

Parents who learn to accept their children exactly as they are without projecting their own desires and hopes onto them raise children who are sovereign, joyful beings. Moreover, teaching children that whatever feelings may arise within them are valid and are meant to be fully felt, guides them toward emotional intelligence.

Children should be taught not to fear their feelings that are deemed unpleasant, and instead to experience them without resistance while trusting that they are temporary. Children who are forced to suppress their feelings because they trigger fear in their parents experience intense frustration. Parents who never learned how to process and manage their own feelings are uncomfortable when their children have big feelings. This creates a legacy of resistance, rebellion, anxiety, and anger.

Refusing to allow a child to feel angry, jealous, or sad actually causes those feelings to fester and become stuck. As long as such feelings remain unexpressed and unprocessed, the child may feel ensnared. This limited worldview creates a trap for a child that may linger throughout their life.

Children are empowered when they discover that all of their feelings can be experienced in a neutral way. When children understand that they can witness, accept, and tolerate any feeling that arises without taking it out on anyone else, that feeling can be processed naturally. Eventually, it loses its power and simply dissipates. **The goal is to allow the child to experience their experience without reaction or resistance.**

This is how drama, which occurs as a result of unprocessed emotions, is avoided. Drama results when a person has not learned to cope with, and to tolerate, their own emotions. As a result, when they are triggered by an external event or by the actions of another person, they immediately dump their feelings onto others, often through the process of blame. This inevitably creates drama because the recipient of these raw and unprocessed emotions is likely to also become triggered. This in turn creates a chain reaction that often gets out of control.

Unknowingly, drama is often used to avoid and distract a person from experiencing their own feelings. Drama can be avoided by engaging in mindful practices such as pausing and breathing. Whatever has arisen should be accepted, noticed, and tolerated without judgment. It is wise never to speak or react until the emotional charge associated with the feeling, such as anger, has passed. In doing so, a person can then choose whether to speak their truth or to simply let it go.

The willingness to experience whatever feeling is triggered in the present moment, without an agenda and without concern for a specific outcome, is the mindful path. Everyone experiences the full spectrum of feelings, and the only thing over which anyone truly has control is their response to their feelings.

Sadly, most people spend decades trying to control external events in their lives. However, the ability to do so is an illusion. Those who tend to feel anxious are usually mired in the belief that worrying will somehow magically keep them safe. Nothing could be farther from the truth. **The only true control a person has is over their own mind. The work of mindfulness is to** *mind one's mind.*

True joy is found in the knowledge that one can tolerate *all* of their feelings. Sitting with feelings without reacting to them and without blaming or projecting fault onto another are essential to living a mindful life. Teach this to a child and they will be able to live comfortably within themselves and find their way in the world.

Many parents force an agenda onto their children, fearing that if they do not, their children will fail in the world. When a parent allows their child to see who they are meant to be, the child learns to act freely in the present moment without feeling burdened by the parents' needs and desires.

With this freedom comes permission to experience all feelings that arise without the need to react to them. When a child is not afraid of a parent's reaction if they are upset, or if they fail at a task, they are more likely to be open to trying new things and taking reasonable risks.

Children are human beings, not human doings. While children should not be forced to meet a parent's agenda by being busy with activities every moment, this is not intended to suggest that children should be allowed to sit around doing nothing. When a parent accepts their child's nature without placing onerous burdens on them to satisfy their own fantasies concerning the future, it allows the child to experience life as it comes at them.

In turn, the child will feel free to try new things if offered a voice in determining their interests and passions at any given age based on their developmental stage. This in turn creates internal motivation which lasts a lifetime. True motivation can only be generated internally. External pressure causes fear, resentment, and anger. Ironically, it also causes resistance which can present as laziness. **What a parent fears is likely to manifest.**

Acceptance of the entire spectrum of feelings is necessary in order to understand and process those feelings. Just as a big meal has to be digested to avoid feeling heartburn, so too do emotions have to be digested in order to avoid "soul burn."

Teaching children to experience whatever emotions they are feeling without fear allows them to move through those feelings with greater ease. Demanding that a child avoid expressing all of their feelings, regardless of how uncomfortable they may make their parent, is a great disservice to the child.

The full breadth of human emotions can be compared to the ocean. At times, the ocean is calm, at other times it is choppy, and sometimes it is ferocious. However, none of these states are permanent. Similarly, feelings can be likened to waves in the ocean, and a strong feeling can be thought of as a strong wave. The first step in processing any feeling is to notice and label it (e.g., I am feeling sad, angry, jealous, or furious).

The next step is to honor that feeling by accepting it without resistance or outward reaction. It should simply be observed and experienced while focusing on one's breath. The intention is to feel the feeling completely and surrender to it. It can be thought of as surfing the wave rather than drowning in the ocean.

When you imagine that a feeling is like an ocean wave, you can watch it slowly gain power and momentum, after which it will crescendo and then dissipate. While surfing the wave of your emotion, it is important not to feed it with thoughts, especially negative self-talk or angry judgments. Rather, the work is to experience the feeling with as quiet a mind as possible. People who do not learn this skill tend to get stuck in the emotion as it does not pass.

An emotional wave is often triggered by a thought. The more a person learns to detach from their thoughts, the more easily they will be able to process their feelings as they arise. **Thoughts are merely conditioned constructs and reflexive habits.** They often become the fuel which feeds the feelings.

People often get stuck in a particular state of mind where they are unable to process, move through, and get beyond their emotions. Since many adults do not know how to process the breadth of their emotions without fear or resistance, they fail to teach this critical life skill to their children. This is why the work of raising children is actually the work of raising parents.

Children ought to be taught that all of their feelings are worthy of attention and are not to be feared, ignored, or avoided. When parents learn to allow their children to sit with their emotions, even those labeled as "bad" or "negative," without getting involved in any associated drama and without trying to change their child's emotions or experience, children learn to trust that all feelings are safe.

This challenging process requires the parent to remain neutral and non-reactive regardless of what their child is experiencing. The parent's job is to stay in the energetic space with their child, acknowledging their feelings without trying to change them. This is often referred to as the practice of "holding space," where the parent is present and engaged with their child but is neither trying to manipulate or change their child's experience nor becoming mired in the emotion with them.

Eventually, with patience and practice, this skill becomes more reflexive and habitual, and in turn, a child learns to process their feelings more seamlessly. This is true even for huge emotions that seem overwhelming and feel like a tsunami. These too should not be resisted, knowing that even the strongest ocean wave will eventually recede.

Feelings are just feelings. They need not be imbued with so much power and they will not kill anyone, although they surely hurt. Ironically, allowing children to feel them provides the best exit from them. **The only way out is in! The truest path to emotional intelligence is teaching children that they can endure all of their feelings and that their feelings are temporary.** These essential mindful life lessons teach a skill that will be available to children throughout their lives as they learn that they can handle whatever comes at them without fear, and with confidence and equanimity.

The work of building emotional muscle and strength is as important as any exercise routine. It teaches children to flow with life rather than to resist it. Nature is wise and offers many lessons about flow, surrender, and impermanence.

People often lack the knowledge or insight to flow with their circumstances. This is why life can become difficult, and at times even overwhelming. Once parents, and in turn their children, learn to flow with their feelings rather than either to resist or wallow in them, they will suffer less. This is one important key to living a joyful life in each and every moment.

Taming the Green-Eyed Monster

> *During one festive holiday, Leah, mother of ten-year-old Ariana and twelve-year-old Rachel, prepared a feast and was delighted that the entire family had gathered to celebrate the holiday. Rachel began to recite the ritual prayers with beauty and grace. Leah was enjoying the moment and grateful for the embrace of family.*
>
> *To her surprise, at that very moment, Ariana interrupted the prayers and began ranting about how much she hated her sister. Leah had always prided herself on the close, loving bond that her daughters shared. Naturally, she felt confused, stressed, and embarrassed by this outburst, quickly becoming angry that this beautiful family moment had been interrupted by this rant that arose seemingly out of nowhere.*

In order to try to fix this situation quickly and to stop Ariana from expressing such unpleasant sentiments, Leah instinctively started to compliment Ariana. She wanted Ariana to feel better about herself so she would be quiet but the child would have none of it. As Leah's stress level escalated, she switched strategies and began to reprimand Ariana for her unkind words toward her sister. Neither approach worked.

Leah realized that she needed to engage an unconventional and counterintuitive approach to support Ariana in that moment. She took a deep breath and paused. She then told Ariana that she had every right to hate her sister, that she was not surprised by this outburst as she had expected it to happen eventually, and that she completely understood her feelings.

As Leah welcomed Ariana's feelings of enmity towards her sister, it allowed Ariana to share more feelings she had about Rachel. Ariana told her mother that she could never compare to Rachel who was good at so many things. Rachel looked at her mother in disbelief, but Leah continued to allow Ariana to express her hatred of her sister.

Meanwhile, Leah told Rachel that this had nothing to do with her and that she should completely ignore Ariana's rant. Leah realized that the other family members were unable to tolerate this unprovoked outburst and her response, so she removed Ariana from the dinner table in order to be free to handle the situation mindfully.

Leah and Ariana went to another room where Leah embraced her and began to acknowledge her feelings fully. Since Ariana is an avid reader and a Shakespeare aficionado, Leah asked her if she had been possessed by the "green-eyed monster." Ariana acknowledged that she was feeling terribly envious of her sister. Leah told Ariana that her feelings were totally natural, and she allowed her to express them without interruption or resistance.

Once Ariana started to calm down, Leah gave paper and crayons, and invited her to continue her tirade with words or pictures. Leah also told her that she completely understood why she hated her sister and that she had every right to do so. She told her she did not even have to rejoin the family at the dinner table, after which she hugged Ariana and left her alone.

Leah's family was incredulous. They had never seen a parent indulge a child's jealousy so intensely, especially when it was directed toward a sibling. Leah urged them to withhold judgment. After cleaning the dinner dishes, Leah asked the family to reconvene at the table and watch the magic happen.

At that point, Leah announced "dessert" loudly enough for Ariana to hear from the adjacent room. Ariana immediately ran into the dining room and approached Rachel. She gave her sister a huge kiss on her cheek and said, "I love you." Then she joyfully asked if everyone wanted to hear her sing, and she began belting out her favorite songs, holding a spoon as her microphone. Her joy was unabashed and contagious. Naturally, the *family was delighted and relieved to see that this wave of emotion had passed.*

Ariana had been allowed to fully metabolize her feelings of envy and jealousy toward Rachel without restraint or resistance. Over the ensuing years, Leah reported that there was barely an argument between her daughters. As young adults, they continue to share a close bond.

With the benefit of hindsight, Leah has had the chance to ask both of her daughters what, if anything, they remember of that experience. Rachel refuses to believe that her sister ever said such hateful and unkind things about her and has absolutely no recollection of the event. On the other hand, Ariana vividly recalls the incident. Mostly, she remembers sitting on her mother's lap in her playroom delving deeply into the experience of her jealousy. For her, it was a moment of great release and comfort.

While this was a painful moment for Leah as a parent, she was able to detach from her own emotional charge in order to serve her child's well-being. She released her agenda in that moment so that her daughter's feelings could be felt fully. Her non-reactivity made space for Ariana's huge and unexpected feelings without judgment or criticism. The timing was inconvenient but had to be accepted.

Had Ariana not been allowed to fully experience and lean into her jealousy in the moment that it arose, going forward it would have continued to fester, potentially causing longstanding anger, resentment, and discord between these sisters. Non-resistance of whatever arises in the moment is the path to freedom. **Feelings that are resisted persist.**

In order to allow children to freely experience their emotions, parents need to detach from the fear that those feelings tend to trigger in *them*, especially when the feelings are conventionally labeled as "negative" or "bad." Feelings may arise in response to thoughts, external events, or seemingly out of nowhere. Because parents fear their children's unpleasant emotions, they dread when their children express them. If parents learn to tolerate the breadth of their children's feelings and allow them to experience whatever arises whenever they arise, children can learn to metabolize their feelings without fear and ultimately to release them.

In order for parents to understand their own fear associated with emotions which are classically framed as negative, it is helpful to recognize why they feel afraid. Unpleasant emotions (e.g., sadness, anger, jealousy, or frustration) often stem from a sense of lack or inadequacy within the person who is experiencing them. When they arise, they can even cause physical discomfort which people desperately want to avoid.

As a result, people instinctively try to deny and ignore such feelings in the hope they will go away yet doing so actually causes the reverse to happen. Instead, the feelings get stuck because they have not been processed which can result in the creation of longstanding suffering and unhealthy patterns.

Because parents are fearful of their own emotions, they are often terrorized by their child's emotions, and cannot tolerate their child's suffering. This, in turn, causes the parent to try to control the external situation in order to suppress the emotions that accompany it. However, in doing so the parent is serving their own needs rather than those of their child. They are depriving their child of the chance to learn to identify and process their emotions without drama, and of the opportunity to raise their emotional literacy.

"Negative" emotions signal that the person feels something is lacking in their life. When a person feels envy toward another, they can either be inspired to push themselves in new directions, expanding their boundaries, or they can propel themselves into anger, unhappiness, paralysis, and possibly even self-destructive behavior.

The feeling of jealousy is not, in and of itself, either good or bad. How it is handled and processed makes all the difference. A person can use a feeling of jealousy as an opportunity to look within and try to deconstruct why they feel they have less than another, and then can work to elevate themselves to a higher plane, or they can allow the emotion to fester. This is a choice that every person makes. **The way a parent handles their own feelings will determine the type of role model they will be for their child.**

When a child returns from school feeling jealous that their buddy scored higher on a test or did better at a sport, that feeling should be honored by allowing its full expression. This type of situation provides a great opportunity to practice mindfulness in parenting. Instead of telling a child that they are good at other things or admonishing them for not doing as well as their peer on the test or on the field, consider asking them to describe the feeling of not being as smart or athletic.

The parent can also share a childhood memory of when they felt jealous of a friend who performed better than they did on a test or at a sport. Label the emotion as it is and empathize with the child without trying to change anything about the experience.

A parent can say things like, "I see that you are feeling really jealous of Joey, and I get it." Or they might say, "It's hard when your friend does better than you did on the test." Perhaps with regard to a sport, they may say, "It sounds as though you feel pretty badly that you missed that goal."

Rather than projecting the parent's own anxiety about the child's performance, or trying to suppress or avoid the feeling by suggesting that the child should not feel that way, the key is to simply allow the feeling to be expressed. Doing so should not be conflated with agreeing that the child is not as smart or athletic, but merely agreeing with the child's own feeling in that moment that they are not. **Do not try to rescue, fix, or change any feeling.**

An Invitation to Joy

> *Ashley, a 5th-grader, returned home from school distraught. Her mother Dawn asked her what was troubling her. Against school rules, her classmate had distributed birthday party invitations to many of the girls in the class in front of her and did not hand her one. She asked for her invitation and was told directly by the birthday girl that she was not*

invited to the party. Ashley did not understand how a classmate could be so cruel as to distribute party invitations in front of other kids who were not invited. The teacher had not seen this happen and was unaware of it.

Ashley asked her mother to call the mother of the birthday girl to try to get her invited. As Dawn was upset that Ashley had been excluded, this was tempting. Naturally, her first instinct was to jump in and try to fix this problem. Then Dawn paused and took a few breaths to calm down. She realized that she had fallen into the unconscious trap of feeling her child's feelings.

Rather than taking immediate action, Dawn decided to be the antidote to Ashley's angst by remaining calm. By choosing not to engage in the content of the drama, Ashley saw that her mother was okay with this situation. Her mother was the container for her feelings but would not engage in them directly. As a result, Ashley eventually learned to be okay with the situation as well.

Dawn paused and assessed her own feelings around her child's exclusion. In doing so, it occurred to her that while this was a painful moment for Ashley, if it were managed with mindfulness, understanding, and love, it could provide an opportunity for Ashley's growth. Instead of calling the birthday girl's mother to let her know how upset Ashley was feeling or calling the school to complain about the birthday girl's behavior, Dawn decided that this rejection needed to be experienced without any outside intervention. There was no need to rescue Ashely.

Ashley and Dawn talked a lot about feeling excluded. Ashley felt rejected, and her feelings were terribly hurt. Dawn explained to Ashley that people sometimes behave in unkind ways. While Ashley had no control over the choices other people make, she could control the way she felt about, and responded to, the situation.

Ashley cried a lot and was allowed to express herself without any reaction or resistance from her mother. She told her mother that the kids at school were talking a lot about the party and were very excited about it, which made her feel even worse. Dawn was willing to be the container for all of Ashley's sad feelings. She knew it was her job to empathize with her child, and to validate and hold space for her feelings, even sharing a *similar story about her own childhood while remaining completely calm and at ease. Doing so also sent the message to Ashley that this situation was not catastrophic.*

Ashley even confided to her mother that she fantasized that this was all a big mistake and that the birthday girl would apologize and give her an invitation, but of course this never happened. The day of the party arrived. Dawn planned a fun family day at the zoo. There was no mention of the party throughout the day, which came and went without further drama. Once the day was over, Ashley was able to release her sadness surrounding this incident.

Parents often panic when their child is excluded and worry that they will not have friends. In turn, the child picks up on this worry and feels even worse about themselves as they now have to deal with their own painful feelings of exclusion as well as their parent's disappointment. The parent's reaction can also make the child feel that the problem is even worse than it is.

If the parent acts as the antidote by staying calm and not engaging in the drama, the entire experience can be managed. If friends leave a child out, the child is entitled to feel blue. **Just as fire cannot be extinguished by adding fire, the parent should not add fuel to an already painful situation.**

Friends come and go, especially during the developmental years. It surely hurts to be excluded but when it occurs, a better outcome is much more likely where the parent does not panic. A parent's reaction can cause a child to experience the dual burden of their own emotional reaction as well as that of their parents.

This is why it is critically important for the parent not to hijack their child's emotional experience. Often when a parent has difficulty tolerating a child's challenging feelings, their own feelings become triggered. The mindful parent understands the need to pause so they can make the conscious choice not to interrupt their child's emotional experience, and instead to simply witness it with calmness and offer to help their child process it.

Don't Be a Hijacker

> *Grace was excited to attend her new private school. She was a friendly, bright 3rd-grader. However, during the first few days of school, she returned home feeling miserable. She told her parents that all the other kids already knew each other, knew the games, and knew their way around. She also missed her old friends. Grace pleaded with her parents to allow her to return to her old school.*
>
> *At first, Grace's parents panicked. They felt as though they had made a terrible mistake transferring her to a private school. Grace saw how upset they were, which intensified her reaction. She became even more distraught and began to cry, stating that she would not attend her new school ever again. The family was caught in a vicious cycle, as Grace also felt the weight of her parents' worries. This caused her to feel guilty, and to assume that the problem was even greater than she thought.*

Non-reactivity is essential to connection, and the parent must be a role model for this behavior. Only when a parent has learned to control their own reactions can they teach their child to do the same. Grace was burdened by her parents' unhappiness and worry. Her feelings were being hijacked which caused her to feel guilty, yet she also remained unhappy at school for a while but became scared to share this with her parents. Eventually, when the transition eased, Ashley integrated into her new situation.

A situation that causes one person to feel angry may be entirely neutral for another. This is why feelings should not be ignored but should be dealt with internally. Children learn important lessons when their parents do not react, as it preserves their sense of safety and security, while teaching them to process and express their own feelings in a similar fashion.

When a child is excluded from a party or an event, so be it. It is tempting to try to get an invite by calling the other parent, but it is important to consider whether doing so is an effort to assuage the feelings of the wronged child or the parent. Parents do a disservice to their children when they fail to teach them that life will come at them in difficult ways, but that they are strong and resilient.

Digesting a feeling is akin to digesting a feast. When someone has overeaten, their body needs time to digest. If this luxury is denied, then the person will feel bloated, uncomfortable, and can experience digestive disorders. The same is true of emotions. By experiencing and processing feelings, their grasp will ultimately be released. Feelings are transient by nature. Since they wax and wane, learning to be calm in any given moment will create a sense of natural flow. Feelings, like thoughts and actions, ought to be allowed to flow.

Avoiding feelings also distracts and detracts from the present moment. Sadly, the Founding Parents of our nation focused on the "pursuit" of happiness as an American ideal. Ironically, pursuing happiness can actually create longstanding unhappiness and anxiety. This pursuit may also create cravings that are not in accord with a person's current reality.

Instead of teaching children to pursue a particular feeling in order to live a good life, it would be better if children were taught to be present in whatever feeling they experience in a particular moment. The lesson to teach is that they can tolerate any and every emotion that arises with equanimity and neutrality.

The relentless pursuit of happiness to the exclusion of other feelings should not be the goal. A child who learns to tolerate the spectrum of emotions can handle what life dishes out with neutrality and composure. The doctor who treats very ill patients will not likely feel happy in doing so, but they might feel fulfilled when they lessen pain or heal an illness.

The goal of conscious parenting is to create meaning, not merely happiness, in children's lives. True joy can be found in the ability to engage with life as it presents itself in all its glory and messiness.

NOTES

3 PROCESS VERSUS OUTCOME

- Can I allow my child to fail?
- How will I cope if my child does not meet expectations?
- What if my children do not succeed in life because I did not push them enough?
- Will my child be able to handle the disappointment of failure?
- How can I teach my child the lessons that stem from failure?
- Can I detach from the outcome and focus only on the process?

A parent's ability to focus on their child's process rather than on the outcome will create a sense of accomplishment in the child regardless of whether there is a reward from an external source. Instead of praising your child for beautiful artwork or lauding their "A" grade, consider focusing on one aspect of their artistic creation by telling them how beautiful their rendition of the sun is, or how proud you are that they studied so diligently for the math test.

Imagine the power in refusing to read a report card or in attending a child's swim meet just to watch how their stroke has improved rather than caring whether they win the race. This sends the message to the child that the point of education and athletics is to learn, improve, and grow, rather than to earn a letter on a piece of paper or to win a trophy. The ultimate goal is to detach from external markers of success. This in turn creates internal motivation in the child that will last a lifetime.

Praise for an outcome-based result can backfire and lead to a life of unhappiness and craving for approval, rather than a life of self-acceptance, meaning, and purpose. While praise surely beats criticism, in many ways praise and criticism are similar as they both create internal feelings of lack. Criticism wounds a child as it makes them feel that they are unworthy and not good enough in their parents' eyes. Praise makes them feel the need to satisfy their parents' desires to meet external goals.

Praise, particularly for an outcome-based result, can actually create a dependence or craving in a child that can never be satisfied. The child grows up seeking approval from a partner or boss, rather than knowing that they are good enough.

While it is important to support a child by letting them know that you are proud, it is better to praise their efforts and motivation, rather than any earned outcome. This also allows the child to learn to cope with failure, which is often the foundation for even more lessons and greater growth.

While criticism wounds a child, praise can create a dependence of its own. This is why the more conscious approach calls for refraining from both criticism and praise. Instead of praising your child for being a fabulous poet, tell them that the poem they wrote is expressive and that the stanzas rhyme well. Be sure they know that the fact they did not win the poetry contest does not detract from the poem's beauty or meaning.

Letting a child know that you are proud of the way they diligently studied for the test without distraction, or how hard they worked out regularly with their team, motivates the child to put in the effort and to accept any outcome, whatever it may be. Be specific about the child's input and the effort exerted.

Thumbs Up

Eight-year-old Isaac sucks his thumb at night. He is careful not to do so during the day in order not to be ostracized by his peers, but he could neither fall asleep nor stay asleep without thumb-sucking at night. His parents were distraught as they believed that he should have outgrown this immature behavior, and because it was causing serious and expensive dental problems.

Isaac's father was constantly criticizing him, threatening to put a nasty tasting fluid on his thumb during the night, and complaining about the cost of the related dental treatment. Isaac's mother, on the other hand, was his cheerleader, constantly telling him that he was getting there, that he was doing better, and that at least he did not suck his thumb during the day. Isaac felt both scared of his father's threats and foolish about this behavior, but he still found it difficult to stop. His mother's cheerleading did nothing to curtail this habit.

Both parents meant well, but they were inadvertently creating the conditions for Isaac to continue this habit. Isaac desperately wanted to stop sucking his thumb, but his father's criticism made him feel badly about himself and guilty about the expensive dental repairs. He was also scared of the nasty taste he might endure if his father secretly carried out his threat while he was sleeping. His mother was also making him feel badly about himself because her relentless cheerleading made him feel that he was disappointing her and that he was just not a good enough kid because he could not stop his thumb sucking.

Both criticism and praise were detrimental to Isaac's best interests. He felt awful about his habit as he knew that he was disappointing his parents and costing them money. He needed to suck his thumb at night to calm himself. Isaac's parents would have been wise to remain neutral about this habit and say little about it. They could have empathized with him about how hard it is to break this type of habit as they understood that it brought him comfort, supporting him by letting him know that they trusted him to stop when he was ready.

A neutral approach by parents is the best chance to stem unseemly or immature habits. These parents' fears surrounding Isaac's habit caused them to behave mindlessly and to unwittingly perpetuate the very problem they sought to control. When Isaac's parents stopped focusing on their desired outcome and instead were okay that it was his process, slowly he was able to give up the habit.

Similarly, the process must be the focus when it comes to extracurricular activities and academics. A parent can support their child's growth by providing the necessary materials and opportunities, and then build in flexibility.

For example, parents can rent a violin knowing that if their child changes their mind about which instrument they choose to study, the violin can be returned for a cello - or even for a tennis racket if that is their preference. It is just as important for the child to figure out what they do not like as it is to learn what they love.

Meanwhile, the child must be trusted and given the space to make mistakes and be creative, all the while remembering that they need to experience their own process in their unique way. There is no checklist in life. There is no pursuit of happiness. There is only the process of living in each moment and accepting things exactly as they are, whether that means exclusion from the party, extended thumb sucking, a "C" grade, or rejection from the team.

Also, parents should avoid expressing to the child the expectation that they always need to do their best as that is a slippery slope which can be both confusing and frustrating. That creates yet another never-ending quest which can inadvertently cause the child to feel that they are never doing quite well enough to satisfy their parent.

It is important to remember that in each moment the child is trying to do all that they can, but their effort can be hampered by external circumstances and pressures. For example, the child who feels ill or has a fight with a friend just before a test may not perform as well as they could otherwise, but that may be their best effort at that moment. Therefore, instead of focusing on the child's "best," let them know that the outcome they achieved is good enough. The parent can say things like "well done" or "nicely done" to express their satisfaction.

Making the Grade

> Samantha, a high-achieving 6th-grader, got a failing grade of 60% on a math test. She was devastated, telling herself that her life would never be the same and that her chances of acceptance at a good college had been extinguished. George, her father, realized that she was much too attached to her grades. He understood that this failing grade presented the perfect opportunity for Samantha's growth. She would learn that grades are not the path to self-worth. Her self-image was very attached to her achievements. This incident was a chance for her to see herself another way.
>
> The night before the next math test, Samantha had a meltdown. George wanted to take a mindful approach and knew that a single math test score in 6th-grade was irrelevant in the scheme of his daughter's life. He suggested that Samantha skip the test and accept a "0" grade, as nothing

was worth this degree of anxiety. This idea terrified Samantha. Finally, she agreed to take the test and attempt to obtain at least another 60%. When she achieved a 70% grade, she and her father celebrated.

George questioned Samantha about what was going on at school. With gentle probing, it turned out a social situation was upsetting her terribly, as a group of friends were excluding her. Her father understood that her feelings of exclusion from this social group were causing Samantha a lot of distress, which in turn was causing her to be unable to focus. This resulted in her making careless errors on her math tests.

Once Samantha was able to express and process her feelings around this social situation, including her sadness, anxiety, and frustration, her math grades slowly began to improve. Even more importantly, Samantha learned that her sense of self-worth need not be tied to her grades and that her father's love was completely disconnected from how she scored on any test.

Since achievement is such a fundamental hallmark of the educational system, the idea of detaching from grades seems crazy to most parents. Educators are harangued by nervous parents constantly asking for special consideration so their children can be given higher grades whether or not they are earned. The shift from using grades as an exact measure of achievement, to using grades merely as a general measure of the child's well-being, is a meaningful step towards conscious awareness.

Grades should not be ignored entirely, but instead should be used as a roadmap for further inquiry into the child's emotional and educational health.

- Are the grades consistently low?
- Have they changed dramatically?
- If so, have they all changed in multiple classes or only in certain subjects?
- Does the child need special help in a single subject?
- Is there a processing disorder that needs attention?
- Are there emotional needs that are not being attended to which are affecting the child's performance?

The goal is to support the child's needs rather than the parent's ego. To do this, the parent must be willing not to react to any outcome that is less than desirable. The parent must remember that anger and punishment will not change the end result but will wound the child.

Also, intervening to fix things sends a message to your child that they are incapable of handling things on their own. It also informs the child that the parent is disappointed in them. This too does not serve the child's needs.

Parents often get triggered and feel anger, disappointment, anxiety, or fear when their child fails to perform well. They crave a quick fix to shield themselves and their children from pain. In doing so, their children are robbed of an important opportunity for growth.

The conscious parent knows that it is in their child's best interest to refrain from calling the teacher to cajole them into giving a higher grade or to offer extra credit. Instead, a conscious parent will allow their child to sit with less than desirable outcomes and learn to tolerate them.

This means that the parent will not intervene as the child endures feelings associated with less-than-ideal outcomes. This teaches the child that they are human, and that some degree of failure is inevitable and okay. The child will also learn that failure is often a great platform for growth and creativity.

Ironically, the more a parent allows their child to be ordinary and to have failings, the greater their trajectory for growth will be. **Reveling in a child's ordinariness and highlighting their extraordinary abilities are both critical elements of their experience as a developing human being.**

Raising a Child, Not a Resume

Deborah, a high-school junior, was very disappointed as she explained to her mother that her guidance counselor advised her to drop an advanced placement art history class that she loved in order to continue in a science research course that met at the same time.

The guidance counselor explained that the science research course would look better on her resume and would serve her well in the college application process. She indicated that since Deborah was a great student and would be seeking a spot at a top college, it was imperative that she complete a science research project to support her college application. Not only was Deborah uninterested in the science research course, but she also had no friends in that class.

Deborah was in a conundrum and asked her mother, Elayne, for input. Elayne immediately said that the choice was easy. She suggested that Deborah drop the guidance counselor! She explained to her daughter that her college admission did not depend on any one class and that focusing on her resume missed the point.

Elayne understood that Deborah had found a subject that excited her and that she had developed a special connection with her art history teacher. Deborah remained enrolled in the art history course and dropped the science research class.

Ultimately, having taken art history, Deborah was able to get a volunteer internship at The Metropolitan Museum of Art during her senior year in high school. While she loved the internship, and she excitedly reported to her family that she had worked in a back room filled with original Monet paintings which were not on display to the public, she realized that she did not want to pursue the field as a career.

That was a crucial life lesson for Deborah. The internship created a wonderful memory and helped direct her professional life. When completing her college applications, Deborah wrote an impressive essay about a Bernini sculpture she had studied in her art history course. Needless to say, Deborah was accepted into a good college.

Parents are raising children, not resumes. Each child is a unique human being whose interests and needs matter more than any conventional paradigm based on cultural expectations. If Deborah did not get into a particular college because she had not done a science research project, that was just fine with her parents.

The college application process, like many other endeavors in life, is multifactorial. Trying to pursue certain activities in order to increase a child's chances of acceptance misses the point of education.

Parents often get stuck in fantasies about what they believe will make their children happy, such as attending a particular university, pursuing a certain career, getting married, or earning a lot of money. These are illusions based on parents' desires and entrenched patterns, and often on their own unmet needs and unfulfilled longings. These wishes tend to be achievement-based. Instead of helping their children, they create barriers to their child's independent growth and development as a sovereign human being.

The reality is that learning to flow with life without planning every step, and allowing the process to unfold naturally, is the path to freedom and joy. This does not mean that a parent should sit idly by and do nothing. Rather, they should recognize that there is no single path to happiness. This awareness will allow the parent to discern when to take informed action and when to step back, which leaves room for growth and flexibility.

Rather than trying to game the system and figure it all out for their children, the parents' goal should be to raise confident, content children who can handle life's complexities. This is the path to raising children who will thrive and travel far in life with humble confidence and gratitude.

A Swing and a Miss

> *Alex and Andy, twin fifteen-year-old boys, are great athletes. Baseball is their favorite sport and they have been playing on local teams throughout their lives. Playing on their high school varsity team was their ultimate goal. They worked out tirelessly and practiced intensively prior to tryouts. Both felt that tryouts had gone well, and they expected to be selected for the varsity team. When the list was posted, they learned that Alex had made the team, whereas Andy was rejected.*

This caused the family to spiral into crisis. Kevin, their dad, was furious. A sports enthusiast, he pushed Alex and Andy to excel. He wanted to transfer his sons to another school and to reprimand the coach because of this situation which he found untenable. Not only was Kevin angry, but Andy was embarrassed to have been rejected as most of his friends had also made the team. Andy was trying to be excited for Alex, but he was too sad, so he shut down and refused to talk about his feelings. Alex felt terrible for his brother, but he was also angry that he could not feel excited about having made the varsity team since his brother was so upset.

Annabelle, their mother, understood that what seemed like a crisis in the family was actually an excellent opportunity for her sons' growth if the situation was handled mindfully. Her first goal was to be there for her boys without spiraling into sadness herself. Annabelle knew that adding to the drama by overreacting would send the wrong message. The boys would think that the situation was more dire than it actually was.

She needed to be the antidote and the container for their feelings. She remained calm and neutral, deciding that being present for her sons was what they needed most. If they wanted to talk about their feelings and reactions, she was present to listen and hold space for them to do so without inserting her own feelings. If they did not want to talk, that was also okay.

She also refused to engage with the school or the coach about the decision. Her job was to help both of her sons get through this trauma and learn valuable lessons. She knew that beyond the turmoil, this incident was a gift if everyone allowed the lessons to unfold.

By remaining calm, Annabelle allowed each child to experience their respective feelings and to express them without judgment. She acknowledged how miserable this was for both of them. Her approach instantly let them know that they were loved deeply, but that their world would not fall apart because of a coach's decision. Neither of them was a victim.

By not reacting, Annabelle sent her sons the message that this was not terrible and that they would get through it. Her non-reactivity also allowed them to see that she was not disappointed in this outcome. She even allowed Alex to share his anger and guilt over the fact that he could not revel in his success.

In the midst of Annabelle's mindful response, the lessons began to unfold. First, both Andy and Alex learned that whatever happens externally need not impact how they feel about themselves. Andy is not any less skilled at baseball because of this rejection. In fact, nothing had changed in his life. He was just left off the team.

Annabelle explained that there are many reasons this might have happened, and it was not anyone's job to figure them out. There are many disparate and sometimes unrelated factors at play in these types of decisions, and there was no need to investigate. It just is the way it is.

The reality now existed in their family that Alex would play on the varsity baseball team and Andy would not, and this is exactly how things were meant to play out. Eventually, with his mother's help, Andy was able to see the gifts underlying his rejection:

- The world did not end because he did not make the high school varsity team.
- He may or may not ever learn the reasons for his rejection, and that was okay.
- Acceptance and rejection are both okay, can be tolerated, and can occur for many reasons.
- He is still a great baseball player.
- He is still an even greater kid.
- No one else's judgment of him ultimately matters as long as he feels worthy.
- Nothing in his life actually changed.
- He has more free time because he does not have to attend varsity practice.
- This decision by this coach was a loss for the high school varsity baseball team.
- He is okay regardless of whether he is accepted or rejected by anyone.
- He can choose to attend his brother's games or not.
- He can be happy for his brother's success because he is feeling okay.

Over time, Alex was also able to see the gifts that this situation afforded him:

- He was excited to have been accepted onto this team.
- He could enjoy his success without guilt.
- He would understand if Andy chose not to attend his games.
- He accepted that this outcome was hard for Andy.
- It was not his fault that he made the team, and his brother did not.
- Being on the team would still be fun for him.

What initially felt like an overwhelming, dramatic crisis in the family actually shifted so that it was viewed as a neutral event. Both Alex and Andy learned to be okay and to feel worthy regardless of whether they played on the varsity baseball team.

This transformation began when Annabelle detached from external measures of her children's success. The boys began to understand that whether or not they were accepted onto any team, they were good baseball players and, more importantly, they would be okay. They learned to neutralize the situation since no specific outcome was needed for both of them to continue their love of the game.

Andy and Alex also learned that they cannot and need not control any outcome. This helped them feel more powerful, and it deepened their connection to one another. They often practiced together in the local park so that Alex could improve his skills for the team. They now understood that their pleasure came primarily from playing the game.

The key for Alex and Andy was their mother's shift to a conscious parenting mindset so that they were able to see their worth independent of any outcome. Eventually, Kevin came around and accepted the situation.

After Annabelle addressed her sons' feelings surrounding this event, an interesting discussion might have ensued that involved asking the boys how each would have felt if they were both either accepted or both rejected from the team. Each of those outcomes would have had a different emotional charge, which offers proof that they were attached to the judgment of others and the outcome. If both were accepted, everyone would have been happy. If both were rejected, or as happened here, one was rejected and one was accepted, then the family was thrown into turmoil.

These boys learned that there are many ways to process this type of situation. Most importantly, they learned that things in life are temporary. The varsity baseball season came and went, and with it so did this perceived crisis. What remained with these teenage boys were the indelible lessons they learned from this situation.

This example provides proof that one's sense of worthiness tends to be conditioned on the judgment of others. This is a transactional way of living that keeps people stuck. In order to take control of life, it is essential that each person takes control of their own emotional response to external events.

This work involves detaching from worrying about any desired outcomes and remaining in a state of abundance, regardless of any outside influence. People often make the mistake of trying to control outcomes, when in fact the only thing over which anyone has control is their participation in the process, including their own emotions and responses.

A touching letter was sent by a principal of a high school in Singapore to parents of students who were about to take final exams. He acknowledged the parents' anxiety associated with these tests but reminded them that among all of the students who were taking the exams, there was an artist whose math score would have no importance in their life, an athlete whose physical fitness mattered more than physics, and a musician whose chemistry mark was irrelevant.

He also reminded parents that if their children scored high marks that would be fine. However, if they did not, the parents should not react poorly as that will inhibit their children's self-confidence and dignity. He suggested explaining to their children that a test is just a test, and that they are cut out for bigger things in life. He asked these parents to remind their children that they are loved unconditionally. With such love, their children could conquer the world.

NOTES

PART 2
CREATING BOUNDARIES: IMPARTING SAFETY THROUGH LIMITS AND CONNECTION

Another essential pillar of mindful parenting is the creation of boundaries. This must not be confused with discipline or punishment. Discipline and punishment are punitive in nature and do not teach children to learn from their own behavior or misdeeds.

Discipline and punishment feed the parents' need for control. They create an atmosphere of authoritative control which is an illusory outgrowth of fear.

Resistance to whatever arises in the present moment is grounded in fear. This fear usually stems from the parents' own internal wounds, developed during their childhood. Resistance creates separation and inevitably causes arguments between the parent and child, not unlike a tug-of-war where each side is fighting, and no one wins until one side is exhausted. This approach to parenting creates disconnection.

On the other hand, boundaries provide a framework for holding a line premised on self-awareness and the best interests of the children. When boundaries are clearly set and properly maintained, they should not involve a struggle between parent and child.

Natural consequences should be allowed to flow from a violation. Boundaries can actually empower children and send a loving message as they enhance connection between parent and child. Fair and clear boundaries that are properly reinforced in a family can free parents to enjoy their relationship with their children as they avoid resistance, which is consuming and exhausting. A child's input in setting boundaries, where age-appropriate, helps to empower them. Boundaries, properly set and implemented, are yet another way a parent can show unconditional love to their child.

Punishment makes a child feel angry, unworthy, and ultimately out of control. Often the sanction imposed by the parent is disconnected from the behavior of the child. As a result, punishment teaches no valuable lessons. Instead, it can be confusing and infuriating to the child, actually promoting disconnection and dysfunctional behavior.

Because punishment does not teach lessons and instead makes kids feel angry, children often end up repeating the behavior for which they were punished. In doing so, they frequently choose to sneak behind their parents' backs. Children sneak and lie because they know they will get punished if they are caught. **A child can only be as honest with his parent as that parent allows.** It is the parent who sets the conditions for honesty in the home.

Ironically, parents tend to believe that they must correct and lecture their children in order to teach them essential life lessons. The opposite is true. A mindful approach is counterintuitive to the typical parenting approach, but so much more effective.

Neutrality, connection, and acceptance are more effective and powerful parenting tools in shifting behavior than correction, resistance, lectures, and punishment. They allow the child's authentic voice to emerge. Where connection is developed early in the parent-child relationship, there is less need to admonish or reprimand children as they grow up because they know intuitively what behavior is acceptable.

Laying the foundation for deep connection through mindfulness early on creates mutual understanding of acceptable and unacceptable behavior. Children who have internalized essential boundaries, and been given freedom of expression, have little need to defy their parents.

Parents often question this paradigm as they see it as a hands-off approach that allows the child to rule the roost. This is neither the intention nor the case. Mindful parenting is not without rules, and children are not merely allowed to run amuck. **Respectful parenting honors the child's true essence and authentic voice while imposing necessary limits on behavior.**

The basic principle is that the parent and child are not in a hierarchical relationship where the parent must be obeyed simply because they are the adult. The parent-child relationship should be treated as a partnership where the parent is the guide and teacher. The parent's objective should be to listen to the child and allow the emergence of their unique voice and spirit, rather than imposing conditioned expectations authoritatively. The standard parental knee-jerk approach of "do it because I said so" is both ineffective and mindless. **The only person a parent should discipline is themselves. The only reactions they must control are their own.**

4 ESSENTIAL BOUNDARIES

- What values am I trying to inculcate in my child?
- Is the boundary I have set for my child necessary for their growth?
- Whose interests am I serving in setting this boundary, mine or my child's?
- Why is this boundary important to me?
- Am I willing to be consistent in maintaining this boundary while remaining calm?
- Is my child able to uphold this limit based on their developmental stage and age?

Different types of boundaries should be considered when trying to parent wisely. There are those which are non-essential and therefore can be trespassed when the situation calls for flexibility. Then there are other boundaries that are essential, and their enforcement must be set in concrete without drama. The key is that the parent must be clear about these different types of boundaries, and then must be willing to hold to these standards without wavering.

Parents should say "yes" to their children early and often. There should be as few rules imposed in the household as possible. However, once the parent has chosen to say "no" because this will serve their child's best interests and will uphold the family's values, they must hold that line clearly and firmly.

There are times when a parent needs to respond to a child directly in order to have the necessary impact. The word "respond" is stressed rather than "react" because it indicates that the parent has taken a thoughtful approach to the situation and is not merely reacting impulsively based on their own fear and need for control.

Discerning when to respond to a child with a loud, clear voice and/or to reprimand requires the parent to be finely attuned to the particular child. There are moments when a child must be contained. Knowing when to do this is key. The first step requires the parents to decide what boundaries are essential to their family.

Once these are clear, then the parents can respond to the child in order to help them grow, not merely because they feel justified in exploding when they are angry. While this approach seems counterintuitive to conventional parenting, it is the way to serve the child's greatest interests as they learn instinctively how to behave. Punishment creates short-term compliance out of fear, rather than long-term growth.

Most essential or "stone" boundaries are universal and include:

- Safety
- Education
- Hygiene
- Self-care
- Respect for self
- Respect for others
- Responsibility for one's actions

In some families, there may be additional boundaries that are deemed to be essential, such as religious affiliation and practices, nutritional guidelines, or political affiliation. It is critical for parents to determine the nature of the absolute rules in their own family, and then to understand that all other rules require greater flexibility.

Line in the Sand

> *Tony is a seven-year-old boy whose father Henry is a strict vegan. Tony liked to tease and cajole his father to try to get him to eat foods that are not vegan. Tony does this to try to exert control over his father and to get his father's attention. However, Henry's choice to be a vegan is an essential boundary for him both for his health and due to environmental concerns. Tony needs to learn to respect his father's food choices.*
>
> *This involves teaching Tony the important lesson of respect for someone else's essential boundary; in this case his father's decision about his food preferences. While Henry does not punish Tony for his behavior, he calmly and clearly tells his son to stop interfering in his food choices. Tony realizes that this is an important boundary for his father, and also that he too can create such boundaries for himself.*

When boundaries are clear to children and are not too onerous, children receive unambiguous messages about how they are expected to behave. This provides the child with a sense of safety. Naturally, rules should be in line with the child's developmental stage so that they are able to understand and follow them, otherwise they will be ineffective and cause confusion and frustration.

Children crave essential boundaries that are lovingly and consistently imposed. Within those limits, children should be permitted to express themselves and make mistakes without fear of punishment. The home then becomes a safe haven from the pressures of the outside world. This is a great gift to a child.

On-Call

> *Eight-year-old Joey craves the attention of Scott, his father, who is a surgeon. When Scott returns home from work each night, he often has to take important phone calls after dinner. Joey tries to interrupt these calls by roughhousing with his dad, vying for his father's attention. Joey is testing his father to see whether he is more important to him than anyone who might be on the other end of the line.*
>
> *Joey's mother finds herself triggered and angered by her son's behavior. She feels Joey should know not to disturb his father during these calls and often reprimands him. She also feels that the physical roughhousing between father and son often gets out of hand and borders on being disrespectful. She fears that Joey will feel free to behave this way with other people, and in fact, he has done so at times with his grandparents.*
>
> *Scott realizes that when he receives an important call, he needs to speak to Joey in a stern, calm voice, letting him know that they cannot play together at that moment and he is not to be disturbed. Scott then needs to physically remove himself and enter another room so as not to tempt Joey to continue his behavior. Scott also needs to tell Joey that he will be excited to play with him right after the call.*
>
> *If Scott's call can wait, then in Joey's presence he should inform the caller that he is not available to speak at that moment because he is spending*

special time with his son. This sends a powerful message to Joey that he is most important to his dad.

As with any behavior, before assessing whether Joey needed to be stopped, reprimanded, or restrained, it is important for his mother to pause and breathe as she self-reflects on her reaction. She needs to determine whether it is reasonable to consider Joey's behavior disrespectful, or whether she is triggered because of her own history concerning this type of behavior. She needs to discern why she becomes so irritated by behavior that is normal for an eight-year-old boy.

For Joey, it was joyful to play with his father in this way, especially as he missed him when he was at work all day. His mother realized that she should not interfere. With Scott's permission, Joey should be allowed to climb on his dad's back and roughhouse as long as Scott is comfortable with this type of play.

In this situation, it was important for Joey's mother to step back and allow the men in her life to work this out together on their own. Her need to control the situation was actually spurring Joey to behave even more roughly. She noticed that Joey often surreptitiously looked to her to see if she was annoyed by his behavior. He seemed to feel triumphant when she was irritated, as this was yet another way to capture her attention. For these reasons, his mother realized that she needed to neutralize her response and remove herself from the situation. Scott was more than capable of managing Joey.

Just as connection and boundaries in the home are important to a child's healthy development, schools need to support families by utilizing mindful practices in the classroom. Due to the advent of rigid test standards and measures, along with large classroom sizes and limited resources, it can be challenging for teachers to engage conscious, counterintuitive techniques as they require a great deal of training, self-reflection, and patience.

It is often easier for teachers and parents to resort to rewards and punishments as tools to control children's behavior. Such standard approaches inadvertently reinforce the very untoward behavior they seek to stop by failing to create internal motivation and self-esteem.

Prize and Punishment

> *Eli, a six-year-old 1st-grader, is a smart, capable boy whose emotional development lags behind his academic ability. He is often unable to tolerate his emotions. especially when he is frustrated and not getting enough attention at school. He tends to have physical outbursts which frustrate his teacher. He calls out in class, and even kicks and elbows his fellow students at random. His peers are starting to avoid him. His loving mother is horrified by his behavior and has tried every punishment to control his outbursts, all to no avail.*

Eli's teachers began a program in class in which they dispense tickets to each child every Monday. Throughout the week, the children lose tickets if they breach rules or exhibit "bad" behavior. At the end of the week, the teachers dispense prizes to those students who have tickets left, and the type of prize depends on how many tickets are left. For months, Eli never earned a prize. In fact, at times Eli owed extra tickets back to his teachers as he lost more tickets than his weekly allotment. Eli was actually in debt!

Eli's parents were terrified of this ticket program because their son never won a prize, and it highlighted his poor behavior. Eli was only bothered by it because he saw his parents' distress. At first, he was punished at home when he lost tickets. Over time, his parents began to see the flaws in this type of reward-punishment program which relied on external measures to control children's behavior.

Eli's parents began to understand that in order to serve Eli's highest self, they needed to detach from their feelings about this ticket program and make it a non-issue in their home. If Eli lost his tickets and did not earn a prize at school, so be it. When Eli earned a prize, the moment was marked simply with a high-five, but not celebrated with a parade.

Over time, as Eli's mother learned to control her fears about her son's aggressive behavior and consequently her reaction to him, Eli began to calm down. She realized that he acted aggressively when he became excited since he could not figure out how to express or contain himself in those moments.

His mother worked with him on new ways to express his excitement, wait his turn, and get the attention he desired. He learned to pause and breathe when he was excited, and to salute, high-five, and raise his hand rather than be physically aggressive. This new behavior became habitual, and his behavior improved dramatically.

There are significant problems in using a reward and punishment approach to controlling children's behavior. While it may seem like a useful approach in a classroom when it comes to controlling behavioral problems, in a student like Eli it actually made his behavior become even more entrenched.

By its very nature, it creates comparison and competition among classmates, teaching students to rely on external measures to control their emotions. As a result, it hampers their ability to learn how to self-regulate.

As Eli matured emotionally and learned alternative responses, he was able to control his behavior. In turn, he was able to sustain friendships, which motivated his desire to behave more in accord with the school's expectations.

Ironically, perhaps Eli would have been well-served by getting extra tickets for every tantrum. The more tantrums, the more tickets! Naturally, this humorous idea is intended to highlight the fact that efforts to control Eli's behavior through prizes were actually having the opposite impact by causing him to act out more.

When he elbowed a peer who in turn refused to have a playdate with him, it served him well to suffer the consequence. His mother realized this and stopped urging the other parent to reconsider. Instead, she allowed Eli to be sad and lonely. When he was forced to experience the natural consequences of his behavior, he learned to control his reactions.

Eli's mother started to see that her inability to tolerate his behavior worsened it. Deconstructing why this triggered her so much, she realized that she had been a compliant child and had always been rewarded with praise for her "good" behavior, which made her son's "bad" behavior so intolerable to her. As she began to manage her fears around Eli's impulsive outbursts, his behavior improved.

What Eli's teacher did not anticipate was that this ticket program, which was implemented in an earnest effort to control the behavior of their young students, actually caused untoward and unhealthy consequences for many of their students. Each was suffering from this paradigm, albeit in different ways. It did nothing to create tools for the children so they could learn how to self-regulate. Neither did it promote their internal self-confidence or self-control. Instead, it caused many problems for them over time. For example:

- More compulsive and nervous children felt panic about losing tickets, which caused undue anxiety.
- More capable and emotionally mature children who regularly won prizes felt superior, which caused them to become arrogant.
- Controlling, fearful parents punished their children when they did not earn prizes, which caused those students to become angry and lessened their self-esteem.
- Emotionally immature children felt sad and dejected when they could not control their actions and consequently did not earn tickets.
- Students like Eli simply stopped trying to earn tickets and claimed that they did not care about winning tickets, although internally they were distraught about disappointing themselves and their parents.
- Students like Eli who could not earn tickets were getting used to losing and stopped trying.

Rewards and punishments only provide short-term results and are outcome-based. In order to inculcate longstanding internal motivation in children to follow rules and abide by societal norms, *connection* is always paramount.

Begging for Boundaries

> *Janice is the mother of three teenage boys. While she is a sweet, kind, and friendly woman whose sons function well in many aspects of their lives, they are extremely rude to her and her husband. They snipe at her and say unkind things, at times calling her "stupid" and at other times ignoring her entirely. They also refuse to help around the house with basic chores, to honor basic rules around devices, and to talk to her about their lives. Janice is frustrated. Her husband has no idea what to do, so he ignores the problem.*

> *Janice and her husband do not realize that their parenting style is actually reinforcing their sons' ugly behaviors. While they were adamant that the boys follow non-essential, soft rules like not eating in their*

bedrooms, they failed to address their perpetual rudeness, allowing this essential boundary to be violated repeatedly without consequence.

After digging more deeply into how this behavior developed, Janice realized that she tolerated this behavior in her sons because she was too timid to address it. She had allowed this boundary of respect and decency to be crossed repeatedly by her oldest son, and the younger ones followed suit. As a result, this became their mode of communication and interaction. Janice also realized that in her childhood home, disrespect and abuse were commonplace behaviors exhibited by her father, which is why she did not know how to put an end to it.

Janice realized that as a young mother she had lost connection with her boys while also failing to be clear about essential boundaries. She had no idea that since her sons never felt that their emotional needs were being met with loving connection, they used rudeness to get attention. Connection was non-existent and boundaries were repeatedly crossed.

While it is much more challenging to shift this behavior during the adolescent years, it can be done but requires adherence to a new mindset along with consistent follow-through. First, Janice needed to spend uninterrupted quality time with each child on a regular basis. Also, as a team, she and her husband needed to create new household rules with input from the boys concerning how their rude behavior would no longer be tolerated, although they were assured that their voices would be heard if they spoke with respect.

Janice also began to understand that avoidance and denial were the purveyors of this mess. This was a moment that called for self-compassion as well as consistent adherence to a new paradigm. There was nothing to be gained from blaming or shaming herself. Awareness is the key to change, and she could not change what she was unable to see before.

Unconscious patterns develop in every home. Awareness of these patterns is the first step toward shifting them. First, Janice needed to honor herself for becoming aware of her extreme denial and avoidance, which had allowed this rude behavior not only to be tolerated but to flourish in her home. Since her sons did not speak to other authority figures, such as teachers, counselors, and friends' parents in this manner, it was obvious that they knew better.

It was time for these parents to assert themselves, but they needed to do so without any emotional charge. They needed to remain caring and neutral as they began to understand that their sons were literally begging for boundaries as their disrespectful behavior escalated. Ignoring this level of rudeness was actually a great disservice to their children.

Their work was to get beneath the words and behavior and try to figure out the cause of these symptoms, not unlike figuring out a medical diagnosis. Once they became more attuned to their children's needs, they began to address them.

Janice and her husband steadied themselves as they understood that their sons would rebel and resist the new rules and mores. At first, their teenagers were even more rude and refused to talk to them. Their pattern of communication was deeply ingrained and served as an avenue for release of their frustrations, to which they felt entitled.

Holding back on this rude behavior would not prove easy for them, but it was essential for their well-being. Janice and her husband continued to work toward breaking through the disrespect and connecting more deeply.

It took a long time for Janice and her husband to get their boys to understand that their behavior would no longer be tolerated. However, through consistent effort to connect, over time and with greater maturity, the disrespect finally shifted. **Connection is the transformational agent.** It is always advantageous to reinforce connection earlier in children's lives.

In some families, the absence of boundaries and the failure to follow through when they are crossed can lead to difficult and resistant behavior. This is especially true when this type of behavior has gone on for an extended time. Nonetheless, it is never too late to become more aware and work on shifting even the most deeply entrenched patterns.

NOTES

5 BREACHING ESSENTIAL BOUNDARIES - CHEATING, STEALING, AND LYING

- **What role have I played in setting the conditions for poor behavior in my home?**
- **What message has been communicated which makes my child feel the need to be deceptive?**
- **Has a lack of connection contributed to this behavior?**
- **Does my child's behavior stem from fear of punishment or from anger over disconnection?**
- **How can I reconnect with my child to promote honesty and candor?**

Without realizing it, patterns in the home set the conditions for a child's behavior. Deception and dishonesty are not inherent in a child's nature. When a child behaves in untoward ways, it is the parents' job to be honest with themselves so they can discern how they contributed to this behavior. A child's behavior signals an unmet emotional need. The parents' job is to become a detective and investigate the need beneath the behavior. This requires curiosity and openness.

Just as Janice and her husband inadvertently created the conditions for extreme rudeness and disrespect in their home, all parents create the standards and expectations in the home. In turn, their children behave in ways that meet those standards.

When children exhibit undesirable behavior, such as cheating, stealing, and lying, it is wise for their parents to recognize their own role in co-creating the conditions which caused this behavior. While a parent's knee-jerk reaction to such behavior is to reprimand and punish, a mindful parent should consider accepting responsibility and ascertaining how to shift expectations in the home in order to avoid this behavior in the future. Punishing, yelling, criticizing, and shaming actually ensure that such behavior will persist.

And I'll Lie If I Want To...

Sarah, a 3rd-grader, stormed home from school one day, infuriated and slamming the door behind her. Her mother, Diane, naturally asked her what was wrong. Sarah responded that her teacher accused her of cheating on a math test and consequently gave her a "0" grade.

Diane reacted furiously as her ego was triggered by the teacher's accusation. "My child would never cheat," Diane told herself, believing that she had taught Sarah better values. She then told Sarah that she would call her teacher right away to complain.

Imagine Diane's surprise when the teacher informed her that during the math test, Sarah had surreptitiously opened her math textbook on her lap to look up the answers. The fact that Sarah had attempted to hide her actions from the teacher made it abundantly clear that she knew she was cheating. Diane had to accept that Sarah had both cheated on the test and lied to her about it.

Diane paused and took a breath. While she was upset, she also thought it was funny that Sarah believed she would be able to get away with this even when she knew her mother would call the teacher. Diane also knew that since Sarah was only seven-years-old, she was unable to think ahead and comprehend the fact that when her mother called the math teacher, the truth would come out. Sarah was only able to calculate the immediate situation and figured that her mother would have sympathy for her if she lied about getting caught cheating.

Once Diane calmed down, she knew that the manner in which she handled this situation with Sarah would make all the difference in how her daughter processed it. This moment would either be one of great growth for Sarah if handled mindfully, or it would be one of stagnancy in which cheating and lying would become standard behaviors that Sarah would use to handle stressful situations.

Diane considered her daughter's young developmental age as she responded. She sat Sarah on the couch and insisted that they make eye contact as she gently took hold of Sarah's chin. Diane explained that she had learned from her math teacher that Sarah had indeed cheated on her math test. Diane told her that she was sad and disappointed both that Sarah felt that she had to cheat on the test in order to get a good grade, and then that she was too afraid to be honest with her about what she had done when she got caught cheating. Sarah's chin began to quiver, and the tears began to fall.

Diane looked into Sarah's eyes and told her that she had failed her daughter. The fact that Sarah needed to cheat on a test meant that she was under too much pressure to achieve a high grade. Diane explained that if Sarah did get a high test score because she had cheated, that grade would be meaningless even if no one else ever found out. She made a solemn promise to her daughter that she would never reprimand or punish her for any grade as long as the outcome was based on her own honest effort. It was even okay if she failed a test, as long as she did not cheat.

Diane then apologized to Sarah as she understood that her expectations caused this behavior. Sarah promised never to cheat on a test again since she would never face consequences regardless of her grades. Diane also asked Sarah to trust her enough to be honest with her when her behavior fell short of her mother's expectations.

Upon Sarah's high school graduation, Diane asked her if she remembered that conversation from so many years ago. To Diane's surprise and delight, Sarah responded that she vividly recalled it. Diane's response to Sarah's cheating and lying in the 3rd-grade remained with her throughout her academic career. Diane had kept her part of the bargain, never responding to any test grade, high or low, and Sarah assured her mother she had kept her end of the deal as she had never again cheated on a test as she never felt the need to. **Children are only as honest as their parents allow them to be.**

Children lie and cheat when there are demands placed upon them that they either cannot meet, do not want to meet, or when doing so causes them inordinate stress. Sarah's behavior surrounding that 3rd-grade math test was one of her greatest lessons and Diane was glad that it happened the way it did at such a young age.

This experience resulted in a huge shift in Diane's expectations for Sarah, as she recognized that she was focused on external measures of success, especially grades, without considering her child's abilities and needs. Ironically, over the years Sarah began to study more when she knew that the outcome was of no concern to her mother. Without needing to resist her mother, Sarah's internal motivation grew.

Resistance causes untoward behaviors to persist and become more concretized. Think back to the metaphor of a tug-of-war where both people are pulling at the rope in opposite directions. There is little movement even when both sides are trying so hard to pull the rope towards them and are exhausting themselves. As with the imposition of boundaries, when the parent lets go of their end of the rope, the child on the other end will no longer be in resistance. A tug-of-war between parents and their children creates disconnection and frustration on both sides.

Parents need to set conditions in the home where their children feel safe to fail or to succeed. This can be done when the parent decides that regardless of societal pressures, they are going to set conditions where the children feel safe even if this means not enforcing standard expectations.

While it may seem counter-cultural and therefore shocking when a parent decides to give little importance to report cards, doing so can be liberating as it sets the conditions for even greater academic success and candor in the home. Report cards have become the marker of a child's abilities and well-being, and ultimately a reflection of the parents' ego.

A poor report card tends to make the parent feel like a poor parent, whereas a good report card tends to feed the parent's ego. This confirms that a parent's feelings about their child, and ultimately about themselves, are based on external measures. Imagine removing this external measure and instead focusing on the child's interests, needs, and abilities, while assessing their well-being using a multitude of parameters. It may feel radical to remove the focus on external measures, but it emboldens both the parent and the student.

Parents usually feel compelled to monitor their child's grades. This is not to say that grades do not have a place as part of an overall guide to a child's well-being and ability to meet academic standards. Grades should be used as a measure of how a child is doing and as a tool to help decipher how they might help the child's educational process.

However, avoiding a focus on grades will free the child from the stress of having to perform, which in turn will liberate the child from the pressure of having to cheat and lie. The parent who finds that their child tries to hide their report card should take note that the child is feeling fear and stress.

...But I Don't Need To

> Several years later, when Sarah was in 7th-grade, she returned home from middle school in tears, having scored 50% on a language test. Diane did not react. She simply responded, "Oh, I see" and walked away. Diane allowed Sarah to process the issue on her own.
>
> Without any emotional charge, Diane waited for bedtime and asked Sarah what happened. Sarah responded that she had forgotten to study for this test. Diane gave Sarah a high-five and said that it was incredible that she got half of the test answers correct without even studying, as it showed how smart she was. Then she asked Sarah if she had any idea about how to avoid this problem in the future. Sarah responded that she had been thinking about it all day and asked if she could purchase a new planner.

As children tend to be less guarded at nighttime, bedtime is always a good time to talk about things that happened during the school day. Since hours had passed following the incident at school, the emotional charge for Sarah had lessened. On her own, throughout that afternoon, Sarah figured out how to do better going forward. She decided to make notes in her planner for several days in advance of tests so that she would not forget to study each night.

This happened in the space of openness and non-judgment. Had Diane become angry, and reprimanded or punished Sarah, her energy would have been spent feeling anger, shame, and frustration, rather than in creating meaningful solutions going forward.

Diane's neutrality also avoided the imposition of self-deprecating thoughts in Sarah. This grade did not define Sarah. Also, the "F" grade could not be changed, and Diane had no interest in trying to change it. She would not call the teacher to ask for another chance, nor would she try to rescue Sarah from any consequence that might flow from this grade. Rather, she was grateful that Sarah had been honest about the failed grade from the outset and that she attempted to create behavioral changes independently which Diane would support.

Sticky Fingers

Upon arriving at home, Manuela was shocked when she learned that her six-year-old son had secretly taken a candy bar from the store and hidden it in his coat pocket. Manuela knew that he did not have money to purchase it. She was ready to scream at him, but she refrained. She paused and took a deep breath to calm herself. Stealing was an essential boundary in her family, and she knew the issue had to be addressed.

First, she calmly asked her son where he got the candy bar and he confessed that he took it from the drugstore, explaining that it was his favorite treat, it was within his reach, and he did not have money to pay for it. He also told her that if he had asked her to buy it for him, he knew she would refuse as he had been given many other treats at the zoo earlier that day.

Manuela told him that she understood his desire to have this candy bar, but that they would return to the store immediately and he would have to tell the clerk himself that he took the candy bar without paying for it. Also, he would have to return it and apologize. Her son panicked and said that he could not speak directly to the store clerk as that would be terrifying. She empathized with him and told him that she knew it was scary, but she would be right by his side and she insisted that he do so.

They arrived at the counter and Manuela told the cashier that her son needed to say something. She then stepped back, and he explained that when they visited the store earlier, he had taken a candy bar without paying for it. He meekly put the candy bar on the counter and told the clerk that he was sorry for taking it without paying for it, and that he would never do this again. She was understanding and realized that this was an enormous lesson for the child. She told him that she was proud of him for being honest and thanked him for returning the candy. The child sighed with relief. His mother told him how brave he was and kissed him.

This is a model of conscious parenting. The parent held an essential boundary by requiring her son to experience the direct consequences that flowed from his behavior. She did this without having an emotional, mindless reaction and while showing unconditional love and support. Her child learned a valuable lesson without being demeaned or embarrassed.

Lying stems from fear. Specifically, it arises from fear of telling the truth because the repercussions are too scary. When a child lies, it is because the parents have set the stage for such behavior. Most people, if they are being honest, will admit to having lied about something in their lives because they could not tell the truth in that particular situation. The truth would cause embarrassment, social ostracism, or be hurtful to someone's feelings.

If children know they will not be punished for truth-telling, then the conditions have been set that allow them to be honest when things are less than perfect. When a child confesses about a misdeed, ranging from cheating on a test to eating too many treats, the parent should express pride in their truth-telling rather than focusing on the lie. This is even true for older children whose infractions can be more serious.

Rated "C" for Conscious

> Twelve-year-old Ezra was invited to a slumber party in celebration of a friend's birthday. He was well aware of his family's rule that he was not allowed to watch "R" rated movies. The boys at the party decided to watch such a movie on an iPad. Ezra was torn as he wanted to follow the rules set by his parents, but he also felt peer-pressure as he did not want to be the nerd who was unwilling to watch the movie. He was also curious about it.

> The following morning when he returned home, Ezra's father asked him about the party and what the kids did. He lied to his father and said that they played games all night. Later that day, when he was alone with his mother, she also asked him about the party and he immediately confessed that he had watched an "R"-rated movie. She asked him why he had lied about this to his dad, and he responded that it was because his dad is scary and mean. The truth would have resulted in a scolding and punishment. Seeking to avoid both, it was easier to lie.

> His mother thanked him for telling her the truth. She remarked about how brave he was to do so and how much it meant to her. She realized that the movie could not be unwatched and that there was no point in

yelling at, or punishing Ezra. She discussed the content of the movie with him and asked him if he had any questions about it.

At Ezra's request, his mother agreed not to call the parents of the other boys, knowing that this would embarrass Ezra and that most parents have a difficult time hearing about their own children's behavior when it is less than perfect. Parents often justify or deny their child's behavior when another parent calls to complain or inform. She was aware that she was not responsible to intervene in the relationship between other parents and their children.

This incident also provided a teachable moment. Ezra and his mother discussed what he would do when he encountered more serious peer pressure at parties involving drugs and alcohol during high school. Together, they set up scenarios about this, practiced role-playing, and created a plan where Ezra could send a preplanned text message to his mother which would signal to her that he needed a ride home immediately without letting his friends know why.

Ezra's mother assured him that she was always willing to be the "heavy" to get him out of difficult situations. She also informed him that if he ever needed a lift home in an intoxicated state, he should not hesitate to call her, and he would not be punished. She discussed the importance of never getting in a car with an intoxicated driver.

NOTES

6 NON-ESSENTIAL BOUNDARIES

- Why have I set this rule?
- Whose interests am I serving?
- How important is it that my child follows this rule?
- How will I feel when my child does not, cannot, or will not comply?
- How flexible can I be about it?
- Can I give my child the power to determine whether and when to follow this rule?

Non-essential boundaries constitute all rules that are not mandatory. There should be as few of these soft rules as possible so that children do not feel burdened by a complex set of restrictions. These limits should also be implemented to meet the children's needs and developmental age rather than as arbitrary requirements instituted by parents merely because "I said so." Therefore, these types of rules also need to change as children grow and develop.

The goal is for children to feel that their parents are setting rules that have a purpose, rather than implementing rules that merely restrict children as a means of control. **It is important to get off children's backs, and on their sides.**

Candy Land

> *Dana, a mother of two, was opposed to sugar in all forms. She refused to allow her eleven-year-old daughter, Cadence, any treats containing sugar whether at school birthday parties or family celebrations. In fact, she would send sugar-free donuts to school for Cadence to eat on days when birthdays were being celebrated in class. This was a point of great pride for Dana, as she felt that she was being a better mother than all the others. One day, when Dana went to her daughter's closet to search for a pair of shoes, she was shocked and distressed to find an overflowing stash of empty candy wrappers.*

This was a moment of clarity for Dana. She realized that she had created too strict a rule around sugar intake, and as a result, it had backfired. Her conditioned belief that sugar had to be avoided created an untenable situation for her child. Cadence liked candy and treats, as most children do, and she refused to be tethered to this untenable rule. Instead, she simply chose to lie to her mother and eat candy secretly whenever she wanted, often forgetting to discard the wrappers.

This situation caused several problems. First, Cadence was lying to Dana repeatedly. The conditions that led to this lie had been set by Dana. Second, Cadence became obsessed with eating candy since it was treated as the forbidden fruit. Instead of allowing treats in moderation, this "all or nothing" approach created constant cravings in Cadence.

Dana realized that her response to this situation would create either greater connection with Cadence or further dysfunction and disconnection. After recovering from the discovery of the candy wrappers, she decided to approach Cadence about it.

First, she apologized for imposing too strict a rule around sweets. She explained that when she was a child, her parents refused to allow her to eat any goodies. While she hated the rule, she thought that she had to do the same thing as a parent.

She also told Cadence that she had realized that this strict rule had not accomplished her stated goal, which was to keep Cadence from eating any products containing sugar. She asked Cadence to be honest with her in the future about her food preferences, while she promised not to be critical. In order to reestablish trust around this issue, she took Cadence to the grocery store and bought several of her favorite treats, including candy.

Moderation and flexibility are the keys to implementing non-essential boundaries. It is better to impose fewer rules and to expect that they will be broken at times. Before imposing rules, parents need to think about whose interests they are serving. This always requires the parents to look inward to ascertain whether they are acting out of fear, anxiety, and mindless repetition of their own childhood patterns, rather than in their children's best interests.

The more parents allow children to have a say in the household rules, the more likely it is that their children will follow them. At times, all children push the boundaries. This is their job and their right. When they do so, the parent would be well-served to return to the basic principle of *connection versus correction*. Talk to the child about why they felt the need to breach this rule and then listen. Children will talk candidly if they do not fear reprimand or punishment, and if trust has been developed.

Swimming Upstream

Thirteen-year-old Maddie hated swimming. Her parents had been competitive swimmers in college where they met. They were desperate for Maddie to be a great swimmer. As soon as she was eligible, they signed her up for her school's junior varsity team. The rule in their family was that everyone must exercise daily. Swimming was considered the most acceptable choice.

Maddie attended swim practice at school daily. Although she hated it, her strokes and times were improving. She did not tell her parents how much she hated being on the team, and how fearful she was of the swim meets as they were so competitive. Also, her coach scared her as he screamed a lot. She saw how happy her participation in the swim team made her parents, so she went along with it without complaining. Her parents attended every swim meet and she liked the attention.

Maddie's parents then decided that she needed to join yet another swim team, which was even more competitive, as this would allow her to swim before school as well. They knew that if her times improved enough, she might eventually get admitted onto a college team and get a scholarship, as each of them had done. To accomplish this, Maddie needed to put in more hours in the pool every day for the next few years.

Maddie had to awaken two hours earlier than usual to go to the community pool for this extra practice. After a few days, she was exhausted and unhappy. One early morning, upon arriving for practice, she showered in the locker room so that her hair would be wet, and then she slept on the locker room floor without ever getting into the pool. Several of the girls were doing this and it seemed like a reasonable way to avoid early practice and get more rest without telling anyone. For months Maddie's parents had no idea that she was not swimming each morning.

One day the coach called Maddie's mother to say that she was being kicked off the team because of her poor attendance. Her mother said that there must be some mistake as she was driving Maddie to the pool every morning. Finally, Maddie confessed that she was sleeping on the locker room floor rather than swimming. She explained that she hated swimming but that she was afraid of disappointing them.

Maddie's parents had not realized that they were so invested in seeing her follow in their footsteps that they never bothered to even ask her if she was interested in swimming or if she wanted to swim competitively. At first, they considered punishing her for lying to them. The outside team was expensive, and they were furious that she was so unappreciative and wasted their money.

Her father then realized that this was not Maddie's fault but theirs. This was a wake-up call for them. They had never considered her wishes. They had never even asked her if swimming was a sport she wanted to pursue. Instead, they required her to do this without consulting her despite the fact that she was old enough to have a say in her extracurricular activities.

Her father asked Maddie what activities she would prefer, and she said she would love to take an art class. Her parents agreed and allowed her to withdraw from both swim teams. Maddie was relieved.

This situation called for connection rather than correction. Maddie's parents had finally realized that their aspirations and interests need not be shared by their child. Their need to impose this rule did not consider their daughter's preferences. They apologized to her and asked her to be more candid with them in the future, while promising that she would not be punished for speaking truthfully. They realized that the money spent on swimming was worth it as this was a lesson they needed to learn.

Extracurricular activities are not essential. Children ought to be given choices about what activities they wish to engage in, and how much free time they prefer. While limits can and should be created around screen time in lieu of other activities, children should have as much say in their lives as possible.

Even at the youngest ages, children can express their likes and dislikes, and should be given a voice whenever possible. Imposing unnecessary rules engenders anger and frustration in children, as it did for most parents when they were kids.

Imposing rules blindly is a recipe for disaster. In making rules, flexibility and input are important. When children explain why certain rules are not working for them, parents would be well served to listen and consider whether their child's needs can be met without imposing those particular limits.

Also, as children get older, household rules should be revisited and modified to meet their expanded abilities and desire for independence. Children who feel that their parents consider their input and listen to them are more likely to be willing to follow household rules. Even essential boundaries must be reconsidered as children develop so that they continue to be relevant and serve the child, while remembering that the most essential boundaries, such as safety, cannot be crossed.

NOTES

7 CONSEQUENCES VERSUS PUNISHMENTS

- **Am I imposing punishment out of fear?**
- **Has fear triggered my need to control?**
- **What happened in my childhood that caused my child's behavior to trigger me?**
- **Can I allow my child to experience the natural consequences that flow from their behavior?**

Regardless of how mindfully and consciously a child is parented, there is no doubt that boundaries will occasionally be crossed. It is important for parents to continuously recognize that their child can only behave based on the limits of their developmental age and stage of growth.

When limits are encroached and crossed, sometimes it is because of the child's stage of growth. Whether this occurs due to age, or for other reasons such as peer pressure or the need for independence, the parent should remain non-reactive. This is not to say that the child should be let off scot-free from every transgression, particularly when they crossed an essential boundary. Rather, the point is that the response to the behavior should afford a lesson to the child, while not wounding them.

Tug-of-War

Miguel, a bright 4th-grader, had difficulty completing his homework assignments on time. He would do anything to avoid the task. Sally, his mother, tried many strategies, from offering rewards such as extra video game time, to punishments such as canceling play dates and imposing time-outs. Nothing worked. She was constantly yelling at Miguel to no avail. His continuing refusal to comply caused a lot of tension in the home as it made Sally feel like a failure. The more Sally yelled, the more Miguel resisted. It was a never-ending tug-of-war. The problem was compounded by the fact that Miguel's older sister was a diligent student. She did all of her homework without oversight and on time.

It was time for a sea change in their home. First, Sally had to stop screaming at Miguel. In fact, in order to shift this dynamic, she needed to ignore his homework entirely. Since education was an essential boundary in her home, this was challenging for her as she insisted that homework must be completed on time. Her resistance was rooted in fear as she projected dire future consequences for Miguel. She feared that his habit of not doing homework would cause him to become lazy.

Since nothing was working, Sally finally decided to attempt a more conscious approach. She calmly spoke with Miguel and explained that she was no longer going to be the "homework police." She informed him that she trusted him to complete his homework assignments on time as this was an expectation in the family. If he did not do so, he would have to handle the consequences with his teacher on his own.

Then she asked him how she could help him in this endeavor. They discussed his after-school schedule and agreed that he could have a snack and play for 30 minutes before starting homework. She would set a timer. When it went off, he agreed to begin his homework. Also, she created a quiet, neat space that was reserved only for homework. Miguel told his mother what school supplies he needed. When homework was finished, he was free to have a playdate.

Then the hard work began for Sally as she had to follow through on her end of the bargain and stop questioning or nagging Miguel about his homework. A few days later, Sally received a note from Miguel's teacher that he had not been turning in his homework assignments. This note triggered Sally, but as she grew more frustrated and nervous, she was determined to remain calm and deal with her feelings internally.

In doing so, she realized how her fears were being projected onto Miguel, which was, in turn, increasing his resistance. Instead of reacting, Sally calmly canceled Miguel's play dates and said nothing. Soon thereafter, Miguel slowly began completing his homework and projects on time, and his mother acknowledged this improvement without much fanfare.

Sometimes, despite all of these mindful measures, children continually refuse to meet their obligations. Understandably, this worries parents as they fear for their child's future. Punishment is conventionally believed to be important for a child's future success, but this is dead wrong. Think back to the tug-of-war. **Force never works. Instead, it causes increased resistance.**

The conscious approach calls for the parent to question what was going on beneath the surface of their child's behavior while remaining calm. The problem is more complicated when raising a child whose behavior and patterns are markedly different from those of the parent. For example, parents who report that they were disciplined in school have a harder time understanding and accepting their child's dilatory patterns. This was especially complicated for Sally because her older daughter was consistently diligent.

Parents' historical habits, as well as the patterns of other children in the family, can cause them to misunderstand their child's behavior. Habits that are different from those of the parents, which the parent interprets as "bad," tend to cause the parent to feel angry, scared, and frustrated. Before responding, a parent must first become witness to their internal reactions and then respond with equanimity and clarity. In doing so, the parent should begin to investigate the problem by asking basic questions, such as:

- Is the child having difficulty with the content of the material?
- Is the child unable to keep up with the pace of the work?
- Is the child having social or other difficulties at school?
- Is the child being bullied?
- Is the child unable to sit still during or after a long day of school?
- Does the child have a processing disorder that needs to be addressed?
- Is the child bored with the material?

Often, when an untoward behavior persists, the child has unmet emotional, psychological, physical, or academic needs that have to be identified and addressed. The parent must discern whether the child requires medical or psychiatric evaluation, academic intervention, greater academic challenges, or whether more simple mindful strategies will shift the behavior.

In order for the child to truly understand that their actions cause an effect in the world, they must experience the natural consequences that flow from their misguided behavior. There are usually consequences that occur naturally as a direct result of one's actions.

Too often parents engage in conventional knee-jerk reactions to either protect and/or rescue their child from the consequences of their behavior, or alternatively to impose unduly harsh punishment that scares, angers, and belittles the child. Either of these reactions robs the child of the valuable opportunity to experience the consequences of their behavior, as this is where real growth occurs.

Another benefit of this approach is that by allowing natural consequences to flow directly from misbehavior, the parent is removed as the "bad guy" who is punishing the child. Moreover, there are times when crossing the line does not require any response at all, as ignoring certain behaviors, particularly those that involve softer boundaries, tends to be enough to dissuade such behavior in the future. Where the parent discerns that the child is seeking attention, it may be best to ignore the behavior entirely.

It's All Downhill

> Ted's parents leased a car for him to use to commute to high school as he recently got his driver's license. He had earned good grades and was a responsible high school senior. All of his friends had cars and it was a point of status not to have to ride the yellow bus to school any longer. Ted was allowed to drive one friend at a time in his car, and he adhered to the rules.
>
> However, Ted was lazy about parking near his home. His house was on a hill and his parents never parked on the hill as cars often sped down it, creating a higher chance of a collision. Ted always meant to park on the next block but was often in a hurry and wanted to park on the hill right in front of his house. Despite several warnings from his parents, Ted

continued to park on the hill. One day, right after he got out of his car and stepped onto the sidewalk, a car smashed into his car. Ted's car was totaled but, fortunately, no one was injured.

Ted was apologetic and promised never to park on the hill again. His parents did not overreact and were wise enough to avoid stating the obvious, "we told you so." Ted offered to get a job to help pay for a new car.

Rather than allowing him to get another car, his parents decided that the natural consequence of his behavior was that he would not have the use of a car for the rest of the school year, nor would they drive him to and from school. Ted found himself back on the yellow school bus riding with the younger kids. His parents were wise in requiring him to experience the consequences of his behavior. Years later, when he was able to afford his own car, he never parked on the hill in front of their home.

An arbitrary consequence that does not flow directly from the transgression will not teach the child a lesson. Punishment does not work. Most of the time, the punishment imposed on a child has little to do with the "crime," but everything to do with the parent's need for control.

Punishment, like criticism, belittles children, infuriates them, and ultimately diminishes their self-esteem. This is where the parent must recognize that they should not act in an authoritarian fashion. Parents are ushers and guides, not dictators. Children should never be told that they must behave in a particular way or refrain from certain behavior simply because "I said so," "because I am the parent," or "because I know better."

NOTES

8 WHEN ONE PARENT JUST DOESN'T GET IT!

- Am I willing to maintain a conscious approach to parenting despite my co-parent's unwillingness to do so?
- Is my mindless co-parent hurting our child's self-esteem?
- Can I explain to my child that their other parent is behaving in an unconscious way without demeaning that parent?
- Can I sustain my child's sense of worthiness despite the other parent's damaging behavior?
- Can I avoid interfering in the other parent's relationship with our child?

Parents often ask how to handle situations where one parent is behaving mindfully while the other is behaving unconsciously. The less aware parent regularly unleashes anger on their children and insists on imposing harsh, needless punishments. It is important to recognize that the work of raising one's consciousness is personal.

No one can be forced to learn new patterns and to shift their behavior by looking within. Some people are willing to do this hard work, while others choose never to awaken as it is a scary process. Instead, they often believe that they are right and that there is no inner work to do. This is because this work requires a willingness to step into the discomfort of unfamiliar territory and start taking responsibility for their own behavior.

In life, when dealing with any situation, a person only has three choices - to accept, to leave, or to change, with the caveat that no one can change another person. Sometimes shifts by an enlightened parent may lead to shifts in the other parent (who may be either a partner or co-parent depending upon marital status), as they observe the more mindful approach, but often this does not happen which can be frustrating. Nonetheless, it is always better to have one mindful parent than none.

With that said, as children become more mature, there are times when the behavior of the mindless parent has to be addressed directly. First, the children must be told repeatedly that they can always come to the more aware parent with any concerns about the behavior of the other parent without the risk of reprimand. Thereafter, the behavior of the other parent needs to be explored with the child without demeaning the other parent. This can be a tricky endeavor.

First, the parent should acknowledge to the child that the behavior of the other parent is unkind and unacceptable. Label it for what it is. Then, the child should be asked how they feel when the other parent is unkind, unfair, or makes hurtful comments. Ask the child what they experience when their other parent yells, criticizes, or demeans them. Explain that in those moments, the other parent is doing the best that they can and is acting out of their own habits and history. This does not imply that their behavior is acceptable. The simple fact is that no one can change the way anyone else behaves, not even the other parent.

It is wise for parents not to argue in front of the children, even where the less aware parent feels they have been disrespected. Instead, the children can be removed from a challenging situation while the other parent calms down. Also, if the behavior of one parent is abusive in any way, either physically, verbally, or emotionally, the other parent must protect the child.

Children also should be told that offending behavior by the mindless parent does not mean that the child is not loved by that parent. Rather, it simply means that based on that parent's emotional capability, this is the best they can do under the circumstances. Nonetheless, it is reasonable for both the more mindful parent and the child to agree that the other parent's behavior is troubling and upsetting. Offending behavior should never be excused.

This disconnection by the mindless parent offers an opportunity for the more mindful parent to suggest to the child that they need to make up their own mind about things and figure things out for themselves as they grow up. They can be taught that just because a parent says something does not make it true. Each person is entitled to their own opinion, their own way of seeing things, and their own way of handling things. The child can become empowered as they learn that they are a sovereign being and can decide for themselves whether they agree or disagree with either parent, even though they may have to follow rules imposed by either parent.

Critical Coaching

> *Remember Alex and Andy, who love baseball? Their father Kevin coaches their travel team. As their coach, this mindless dad holds his sons to higher standards than he does the rest of the team. The boys were starting to hate baseball practice as they resented their father's critical coaching.*
>
> *They shared their feelings with their mother, but they were too afraid to confront their dad as he became enraged when he felt criticized. Annabelle, their mindful mother, explained that their dad's reactions and demands were all about his ego and not about them, despite the fact that they were the recipients of his wrath. She also gave her sons the option of quitting the travel baseball team if they wanted, regardless of their father's reaction.*

Teaching children that parental reactions are all about the parent and not about the child is an important lesson. Explain that when a mindless parent becomes uncontrollably angry, it is because that parent has not learned how to handle their own feelings of anger or frustration. Sadly, as a result, they project them onto their children.

A child's behavior can often trigger a parent's anger. The key is for the parent to refrain from reacting to that trigger in the moment in which it occurs. The task is for the parent to monitor their emotional response and determine whether it will serve the child. Once a parent learns of the enormous benefits of behaving in more conscious ways, the parent can hopefully maintain greater equanimity regardless of the facts of the situation.

Inevitably, children will infuriate their parents at times. They break sentimental vases, lose their new jacket, spill the milk, fail the test, and forget to walk the dog. There are an infinite number of actions, inactions, and transgressions unitentionally caused by these easily distracted little people in our lives. Regardless of how the parent reacts or responds, the vase remains broken, the jacket lost, the milk spilled, the test failed, and the dog not walked.

Parents are entitled to express anger and speak their truth to their children, but they would be wise to refrain from doing so until they have calmed down and processed their own feelings about the situation. Before responding, the parent should consider whether they are serving their child by speaking their truth.

It is a good practice to ask themselves whether their comment will create a mess with their child that needs to be cleaned up. If so, the parent should consider refraining from commenting. If there is a valuable lesson to teach, then perhaps a conversation is in order once the emotional charge has passed.

When a parent responds to their child's misdeeds, they would be well served to remember that the child did not misbehave in order to anger the parent. **Children's misbehavior is not intentional.** Rather, their behavior, and the consequences that stem from it, were unintentional.

Of course, where the relationship has become so dysfunctional that the child is furious and out of control, then the behavior is more likely due to the child's deep unmet emotional needs. Remembering that children do not act on their impulses merely to frustrate their parents is helpful, enabling the parents to respond more calmly.

Also, like adults, kids get stuck in conditioned patterns. Just as an adult is not likely to quit smoking merely because their partner or even their doctor nags, begs, cajoles, yells, or pleads for them to do so, the child will not stop doing something simply because the parent has asked many times.

People, including children, are not purposely repeating untoward behavior merely to annoy their loved ones, at least most of the time. Their goal is not usually to infuriate their family members. This is a wise lesson to remember when one parent does not get it and repeatedly behaves in mindless ways.

The reason that people repeat untoward behavior that annoys and angers their loved ones is that they get used to their conditioned patterns as well as the responses that those actions evoke. Even patterns of behavior that people dislike in themselves are hard to change.

For adults, shifting patterns is an enormous task that requires great self-awareness. People tend to crave even their most miserable habits because those habits are so familiar and change is so uncomfortable. Where the mindful parent is aware of this tendency, they can be more supportive, understanding, and neutral when encountering their partner.

It is challenging for parents to shift a behavior when they have acted in the same way for decades. This also explains why the mindful parent is unable to shift the behavior of the other parent, who often does not even see their transgressions. Change requires awareness, and awareness requires introspection which is challenging.

Children also get stuck in conditioned patterns that they repeat into adulthood. When they become parents, they forget how frustrated they felt by their own parents' behavior and go on to exhibit that same behavior with their children, thereby perpetuating the misery of the family legacy. This is why it is so hard to get someone else to change.

Often a parent has to hit rock bottom before they are willing to recognize their role in their child's behavior. Whether the parent who engages in mindless behavior becomes willing to shift often depends on whether they are suffering as a result of this behavior. Such parents are often deeply attached to their way of being and believe that it is right or permissible. They tend to create false narratives to justify their unfair and even abusive behaviors.

Children do not choose to lose their new jacket or fail their test. What the parent needs to realize is that just like adults, children become stuck in patterns that perpetuate their untoward behaviors. In addition, the child may also become accustomed and inured to the reaction that this behavior evokes in their parents. This is why the habitual reaction by a parent can actually set the pattern in stone.

The parent ought to remember that just as nagging will not impact their own behavior, neither will it alter their child's behavior. The child may even derive solace and comfort from the predictability of the situation, as they know to expect the same reaction from the same stimulus. This can be comforting in an otherwise unpredictable world.

The tug-of-war metaphor again provides a good framework to help a parent realize that engaging in unnecessary battles is actually a great disservice to their child. It causes disconnection and reinforces the very behavior that the parent seeks to change. Sometimes a clear metaphor helps a parent wake up.

If a child who has repeatedly been admonished at home and at school for aggressive and unkind behavior is asked why they continue to do these things, their honest response would probably surprise most people. They would probably say that they have become accustomed to the reprimands and they even like them. Being called out is a way to get the attention of parents, teachers, and peers. It is also simply a familiar pattern. Also, change can feel scary.

In order to shift any type of behavior, the parent and teacher should first try to accept and honor the fact that the child is feeding off the attention that they are getting from the untoward behavior. Then the adults need to shift their responses so that the behavior no longer serves the child. This is why continuously nagging, yelling, and punishing do not work.

When the parent continues to react mindlessly, the child is unlikely to shift. Explaining this to the child clearly and neutrally requires inordinate work and patience by the awakened parent. Also, they must consider the child's age.

When a parent speaks from a neutral space rather than a reactive one, it enables the child to hear that parent and understand their feelings. This helps to develop empathy. If a parent thoughtlessly unleashes anger, the child will either shut down or become defensive, which in turn precludes connection. Where one parent really gets it, connection can be promoted even during challenging encounters.

A mindless parent usually cannot tolerate when their child misbehaves and therefore this becomes a source of tension in the family. The reactions of such a parent serve to exacerbate the very behavior that the parent wishes to change.

This is why it is important to teach a child that the reactions of a mindless parent are due to the fact that they have not yet figured out how to control their behavior, although they are surely responsible for it. The child should always be assured that they can express their feelings about their more unaware parent to the other parent when they are angry, frustrated, or disappointed about how they are being treated. Their feelings will always be honored and respected.

Hopefully, the other parent will eventually learn how to handle the child's feelings with greater equanimity and consciousness. This might well develop merely because that parent is losing connection with the child. It might also develop by watching the other parent enjoy a closer relationship with the child. Sadly, it may never happen, and that too must be accepted.

Remember Ezra, who watched the "R" rated movie against the rules of his household? This is a great example of how one parent mindfully responded to the trespass of an important rule. Both mother and son never told the dad what happened. While keeping secrets from one parent is not ideal, they agreed that since Ezra's father would have gotten enraged and punished Ezra for watching the movie, probably by grounding him. Therefore, his mother knew that this was an instance when he needed her protection.

Where parents are separated or divorced, the situation is more complex. Negative feelings between divorced spouses often get infused into their relationships with their children. Parents must avoid involving their children in their marital dysfunction.

Children must be protected from their parents' disputes and dysfunction. This requires immense conscious efforts by both parents to put the needs of the children first. Because parents are often very hurt in these circumstances, it can be challenging to put painful feelings aside while dealing with the children. It is tempting to want to criticize the other parent to the children but doing so is damaging.

No one has control over anyone else's choices and behavior. Instead, the more mindful parent must continue to teach their child about how to handle their own emotions, as well as their responses to the other parent. Sometimes silence is the best response. At other times, role-playing is a great tool to help teach a child how to safely encounter the other parent.

Ultimately, by observing the actions and reactions of the unawakened parent, the child will learn to take responsibility for their own emotions, to remain in control of their decisions and responses, and to understand that they cannot control anyone else. Hopefully, that child will also be able to maintain their self-esteem, having learned that their mindless parent's behavior is neither their fault nor are they responsible to try to change it.

NOTES

9 THE TERRIFYING TEENAGE YEARS

- What feelings are being triggered in me by my teenager's behavior?
- Why has my teenager started behaving this way?
- What is my role in co-creating my child's need to act out and behave recklessly?
- Am I willing to cede my need to control my child?
- Can I tolerate my child's difficult feelings without interruption or intervention?
- Can I allow my teen to experience the consequences of their behavior without interference?

The teenage years present new challenges that often trigger unease, stress, and outright fear in parents. Teens have obtained a measure of independence and are trying to learn to separate from their parents, exercise independent judgment, and fit in. The advent of raging hormones, not yet fully developed brains, coupled with intense peer pressure and pressure to succeed, can often make this an anxiety-producing stage of development for parents and their kids.

The conscious parent of a teenager realizes that these years require even greater connection with their child so that their child continues to feel heard, seen, and worthy, but also greater space for their child to experience their newfound freedom. This is a time when the parent ought to remain keenly attuned to their internal dialogue because their own anxiety and fear can easily become triggered and get out of control.

It is a time to trust and surrender, and to give the child more space and sovereignty while also remaining very present in the child's life. Deep listening is a critical tool to navigate this challenging development stage, all the while remembering that, like everything in life, it is temporary and it will pass.

Break a Leg

> John, a middle school student in California, had a passion for theater and writing. His father Joseph was a serious athlete and sports enthusiast. Ever since John was born, Joseph was looking forward to playing sports with his son, coaching his teams, and taking him to sporting events with friends. John had no interest in any of this. Instead, he preferred to audition for school plays. Joseph's disappointment was palpable, and John always felt that he was letting his father down.
>
> John's mother, Linda, was popular among the other moms in the community and was somewhat embarrassed about John's affect and interests, often making excuses about why he was not trying out for sports teams. John's sense of self was plummeting, especially since his younger brother, Peter, was tall, smart, handsome, athletic, and popular. The contrast was striking, and John often heard his mother boasting about Peter's accomplishments to her friends and family.
>
> John was secretly cutting himself. His parents learned of this when Peter accidentally walked into John's room without knocking and saw open wounds and scars on his legs. Peter was torn about whether to tell his parents as John had begged him not to. Peter felt that this was serious, so he informed his parents about what he accidentally observed despite

John's pleading that he not. Joseph and Linda were horrified and terrified. They had no idea that their son was so distraught.

They immediately took John to see a therapist. The therapist taught John that it was okay for him to express himself in his authentic way, and to enjoy his passions without guilt. John started to heal from the internal and external wounds that had been inadvertently and unconsciously inflicted upon him by his parents through their constant criticism and obvious disappointment.

When it came time for John to apply to college, he decided to apply to theater programs far from home. He was accepted into a musical theater program in New York City, thousands of miles from home, and never looked back. John found his voice and his tribe in New York, where he settled and became a successful playwright and theater critic.

In the teenage years, transgressions tend to get bigger. As a result, they trigger more pronounced and profound reactions in parents stemming from their own anxiety and fear. It is critical that parents remember the lessons of equanimity and calmness during these often tumultuous years.

As a child enters the teen years, it becomes more important than ever for the parent to include them in decisions that impact their lives. A teenager who is required to follow strict mandates and rules without having input will become defiant, rebellious, and angry. All children desire agency over their lives, but never more than the budding teenager. The more the parent has connected with them in the earlier years, and included them in the household rules, the easier this transition will be.

Parents usually feel helpless when they find out that their teenagers are using alcohol or drugs. Sometimes upon learning about this behavior, they ignore it, silently condone it, or actively participate in it. These are not adequate answers. Rather, parents need to step up and create clear boundaries around unhealthy and dangerous activities, as safety is a universal essential boundary. However, nothing will be accomplished through strict punishment. Connection is always the antidote.

Parents must include their children in the household rules and create a safety net when these rules are breached, while making sure that where necessary, they allow their children enough space to safely experience the consequences of their poor decisions.

Often the etiology of bad choices stems from the need to fit in by conforming to social norms. Ironically, the parent's need for their child to fit in and to be popular has been absorbed by the child, who is now a teenager acting out, to the parent's dismay. Now that teen is trying to achieve the very goal set by the parent.

Parents often see their children as representatives of themselves, not unlike trophies. They are seeking reflective glory. As a result, parents have been imposing expectations onto their children, which children often experience as a huge burden. By the time they become teens, they either turn their pain inward and have low self-worth, or they rebel.

When younger children either cannot or do not meet their parents' expectations, they are often regularly punished, grounded, scolded, and demeaned. As a result, when they reach their adolescent years, they do not have a strong sense of self. Also, they often have mixed feelings about their own behavior and their parents' punishments, which can be very confusing. They know they have disappointed their parents, and at the same time, they are angry about the demands placed on them without their consent. **When teenagers have not been honored simply for who they are, they tend to act out.**

If parents are honest with themselves, they have a list of attributes and goals they would like their children to meet and even exceed. For example, they would like them to be popular, friendly, respectful, athletic, musical, and academic, just to name a few. **Most parents want their children both to fit in and to stand out.** In doing so, they set impossible standards. Because of these often unreachable expectations, parents inadvertently place undue demands on their children. Parents would be wise to realize that they probably could never achieve many of the goals they have set for their children.

For children with parents or siblings who have achieved great success, they feel even greater pressure to meet those standards and reach those goals. This is a recipe for disaster, as can be seen in the example above with John. When a child feels increased pressure to meet unrealistic standards, by the time that child is a teenager, they are likely to act out, either against themselves with self-injurious behavior, or externally through defiant and rebellious behaviors.

Cut from a Different Cloth

> *Jody, now a 27-year-old young woman, had a chaotic and rebellious adolescence. By the age of 15, she was hanging out with a crowd of friends of whom her parents disapproved. She was drinking, smoking pot, and sexually active. While she was always a bright student, she frequently cut school and her grades plummeted. Her parents were distraught. They were aware that she was depressed and anxious, and that her behavior was out of control.*

They tried everything to control her behavior, as they were living in fear that she would get hurt, become pregnant, fail out of school, or injure herself. They tried yelling, pleading, nagging, and imposing punishments of all kinds, including grounding and canceling her cell phone, all to no avail.

Jody told her friends that she always felt totally misunderstood by her parents. She described feeling like an alien in her own home, to which many of her friends could relate. Finally, she managed to graduate from high school and enroll in a local community college. Shortly thereafter, she got a job at a bookstore near campus and dropped out of school before completing freshman year.

Jody's parents, who are successful professionals, repeatedly expressed their dismay and disappointment to Jody concerning her choices. They constantly told her how they worried that she would not have a bright future without a college degree. Jody consistently replied that she was happy working in the bookstore and living with her boyfriend. Due to constant disagreements with her parents, she chose to have little contact with them, which disheartened them.

Years later, Jody's mother Adele heard about the concept of conscious parenting and began to study it. She started to understand that Jody was literally screaming for connection and support during her tumultuous adolescent years. She also realized that Jody was trying to find her unique voice in a household where she felt drowned out by siblings who were more compliant and more capable of meeting conventional educational and social norms.

It dawned on her that Jody's behavior had been her only way of trying to be seen and heard, and that Jody could not meet the standards and expectations that had been set in the home, thereby setting Jody up for failure. Inadvertently, they were complicit in her behavior.

Adele realized that Jody was not the compliant cookie-cutter child who could easily follow the pack, and that in turn she had neither honored her daughter's spirit nor met her emotional needs. She also realized that she and her husband had parented Jody through the lenses of fear, anxiety, desperation, and impossible expectations, rather than with unconditional love and connection.

These parents had not engaged with their daughter in an effort to negotiate household rules and try to get buy-in from her, nor had they been willing to listen to her because they were simply terrified that she was not meeting externally imposed goals and expectations. This dysfunction took a toll on Jody, as her sense of power and her special gifts became buried under layers of guilt and unhappiness. As a result, she found it difficult to find her way as a young adult.

Adolescence provides the perfect storm with the advent of raging hormones, budding independence, along with social and academic pressures. This confluence of events often causes kids to want to escape the pressure and simultaneously conform to social norms, which can lead to substance abuse and other dangerous behaviors at ever earlier ages.

While Jody always felt unheard and unseen in her family, compliant children who have bought into the model of high achievement and who have satisfied their parents' dreams of success also suffer under the pressure. As a result, they too are at risk of making dangerous decisions, and becoming anxious and depressed.

Even more problematic is that children, and especially teenagers, often keep these feelings hidden as they do not want to disappoint their parents. These are heavy burdens imposed by parents and reinforced by society. **The work of the mindful parent is to release their children from meeting and exceeding arbitrary goals.** The real agenda is to surrender their own expectations, and focus on the child's unique needs and interests.

Inside Out

> *A high school senior, Sydney, who was among the most popular girls in her class, was also the class valedictorian. In addition to being beautiful and smart, Sydney had done volunteer work with autistic children, was an accomplished dancer, and was dating the quarterback of the high school football team. She was the envy of many of her peers and other parents in her community.*
>
> *One day Sydney confided to her guidance counselor that she spent her weekdays figuring out how to get vodka for the weekend. Getting drunk every weekend was the only tool she had to help her cope with all of the pressures. She was so anxious that her psychiatrist prescribed a cocktail of medications in an effort to control her anxiety and depression, all without much success.*
>
> *What appeared to be the perfect life on the outside was actually the most imperfect situation up close. While Sydney was feeding her parents' egos, the pressure was literally killing her spirit and her self-esteem.*

THE TERRIFYING TEENAGE YEARS 121

Parents often ask what to do when their high school kids are obviously inebriated. They feel scared, panicked, and angry. Instead of reacting, they need to pause, breathe, stay silent, and remain physically and emotionally present, even with their drunken child and thereafter. Ultimately, the goal is to foster greater connection through communication when their child recovers, and that cannot be done if the parent reacts uncontrollably and mindlessly.

Safety is the first and foremost consideration. The child should know that they must never drive while intoxicated or get into a car with another driver who has been drinking or using drugs. The parent must agree to pick their child up regardless of what state they are in without reprimand or punishment. It is essential that the parent sticks to this promise. Otherwise, the child will breach this absolute safety boundary.

Once the child is sober, the parent should try to learn more about what is going on in the child's life. This requires listening without judgment or interruption. If the child is willing to share the circumstances that led to drinking, the parent should not respond. There is an inclination to try to fix and rescue the child, or to express disappointment all of which must be avoided.

Grounding and punishment do not work. Those reactions cause the child to lie and sneak around, while also engendering more disconnection and anger. Underage drinking and drug use are never acceptable and should never be ignored or condoned. Rather, these behaviors must be addressed reasonably, calmly, and mindfully.

Teens should be taught that they need not fear telling their parents the truth in any circumstance, especially when they have engaged in dangerous behaviors. When a child returns home drunk despite the parents' repeated warnings about the hazards and risks associated with underage drinking, the parent has a choice to make.

I repeat that grounding and punishing are unconscious and ineffective reactions. They may calm things in the short-term, but they do not provide long-lasting solutions. Parents should accept that this has happened and open a dialogue with their children about the circumstances that caused it and how to make better decisions going forward.

Teenagers know when they have screwed up. They often act impulsively as their brains are not yet fully developed. A parent should not repeatedly throw their teenager's mistakes in their face. Empathy is the path to connection. **Lecturing does not work and creates greater disconnection, dysfunction, and discontent between parent and child.**

The teenage years are a critical time that will either create deeper connection or greater disconnection between the parent and the teenager. Do not think for a minute that imposing strict punishment will stop the behavior. Rather, it is much more likely that the child will simply repeat the behavior, lie about it, and cover it up.

The desire to punish and ground the teenager is often directly related to a parent's fears. Fear inevitably triggers a parent's need to control, which is disguised, even to the parent, as caring and love. The parent is intent on ensuring that the behavior will not be repeated, but this is an illusion.

The parent who has learned to witness and then tame their own fears under trying circumstances will respond to their child more mindfully, thereby creating more connection. This is the path that may lead the teenager to make better decisions.

One of the most difficult issues in rearing teenagers has been the advent of technology. Teens are addicted to their screens, and their social lives revolve around their use - so much so that person-to-person, face-to-face contact has markedly diminished. Teens who are punished for these behaviors are likely to defy the rules and sneak around. Teens who have a say in the household rules around screens are more likely to follow them. It is important to let the child know that their voice matters.

It is also important for the parent to be willing and excited to spend time offline with a child. Playing board games, taking walks, and having coffee outings are ways to stay off devices while enhancing connection. It takes time to parent wisely, and often the devices act as effective babysitters. Parents must carefully consider whether they are willing to put that time in to create connection.

For middle and high school students, parents should consider creating a cell phone and video game contract at the beginning of the school year. It should include consequences for breaches of the rules that will result in termination of screen privileges. Explain to the child why these rules are being implemented and involve them in creating the terms.

Parents should first question themselves as to the reasons for each rule to ensure that the rule is not being set merely to impose authority and to punish the child. The question to be considered is whether each rule serves the child.

For this reason the child must be reminded regularly that inappropriate photos and behaviors online are dangerous, and that nothing should be said or done online that would not or should not be said or done in person. Children do not have a sense of the future as they are rooted in the present moment. For this reason, it is fruitless to lecture and admonish a child about how images and photos remain online forever and could damage their future. Instead, frequent gentle reminders and open communication about internet safety will have greater impact. Also, the parent must model the behavior that they want their child to follow. A parent who is on their phone, computer, or iPad all evening cannot expect a child to do otherwise. The parent who justifies being online all evening for business purposes is most often using this as an excuse. **Parents should mind the rules or not impose them on their children.**

Parenting teens requires even more patience and connection than during the earlier years. Teenagers will only talk if they know their parents are listening without interruption, interference, blame, shame, or judgment. Their feelings, thoughts, and interests must be honored without criticism. Their physical needs for sleep, uncluttered space, and good nutrition are also essential to their healthy development.

Be mindful that when imposing rules like curfews, there should be room for flexibility. Imposing an absolute curfew can frustrate a teenager. Remember that there is nothing that the child will do outside the home at 10:15 p.m. that they cannot do at 9:45 p.m. Do not get caught up in the details. Instead, create rules that serve the child's healthy growth and development. **The teenager who feels trusted by their parents will more likely live up to that trust.**

A teenager will only trust a parent who has set the conditions for trust and honesty in the home. Teenagers are enigmas as they crave routine as well as unstructured time alone and with friends. A parent who listens carefully will discern their teenager's constantly fluctuating needs. Be flexible and allow for changes as a child grows. **As always, connection rather than correction is the key to parenting a teen mindfully.**

NOTES

PART 3
THE 11TH COMMANDMENT - HONOR THY CHILD

Raising yourself as a parent is the gateway to emotional intelligence and freedom, but the path has many pitfalls and takes great patience and practice. Learning to be a respected, caring, and mindful presence without being a demanding parent is hard work. Honoring our children's authentic and unique spirit is the most important way of showing our unconditional love, and to do this we must honor ourselves, and clear out our emotional landscapes.

This is the way in which parents can instill genuine self-worth in their children. This work is so important to the well-being of our children, and ultimately to our entire world, that it should be considered the 11th Commandment. It all begins with the awareness of how our children reflect us.

10 CHILDREN ARE OUR MIRRORS

- Am I aware of my internal emotional landscape?
- Has my emotional baggage been unwittingly absorbed by my child?
- Can I remain neutral and calm when I see my child acting out in ways that I did as a child?
- Can I acknowledge that I co-created my child's behavior?
- How is my child helping to raise me and serve as my mirror?

Because children intuitively absorb their parents' emotional landscape, they inevitably mirror their behavior. Children are attuned not only to their parents' words but also to their essence, tone, body language, and energy.

It is crucial that mindful parents awaken to their own emotions and patterns with awareness and neutrality. For most parents, seeing their own behaviors and feelings reflected in, and mimicked by, their children is deeply triggering and unsettling.

It is difficult for parents to witness their own flaws being acted out in the little people they are raising. This is why parenting is both painful and rewarding, and why raising children is the pathway to the parent's own growth, healing, and liberation.

Once the parent begins to see how their behavior impacts their children, they can begin the work of cleaning up their own emotional landscape. This is the work of raising a parent.

The emotional landscape encompasses a parent's conditioned beliefs, expectations, habits, thoughts, and feelings. It is reinforced by cultural conditioning. It can be as insignificant as the way the parent handles a minor encounter with a cashier in a store, to the way the parent handles a major life crisis. A parent's awareness of their habits, patterns, tone, energy, actions, body language, reactions, and responses in all kinds of situations constitutes their emotional landscape.

An emotionally intelligent parent is one who is self-aware and can regulate their own emotions, responses, expectations, and behavior. While it is challenging and scary for a parent to look inward and to recognize their own flaws, this is the most important work a mindful parent can do. It is also the greatest gift a mindful parent can bestow upon their child, who inherits their legacy of patterns, feelings, and behaviors.

Awareness is the key to change. A parent cannot change what they do not see. Only after parents shine the light within can they begin the process of transformation. It is only through raising the self, that the parent can consciously raise their child.

Humans behave in habitual patterns. Until they begin to observe those patterns and learn to recognize how longstanding and deeply entrenched they are, they cannot begin to detach from and transcend them. This process requires parents to observe and deconstruct the legacy inherited from their parents, and then to shift and transform. This journey requires a willingness to look inward, and to witness and honor their own imperfect behaviors.

Seeing their own flaws mirrored in their children triggers parents so deeply that for many the process of awareness and change feels too scary and almost impossible. Those who wish to follow this path must be willing to have an open heart, to look inward without judgment or self-criticism, and to want to change.

Self-compassion is an essential element to walking this sacred path. A parent should not condemn or blame themselves, and instead should be grateful that transformation, at whatever stage, age, and place in life, is possible.

Sadly, many children, especially daughters, are burdened with a legacy of self-doubt. Often there is an ongoing internal conversation that involves strongly ingrained thoughts of pervasive unworthiness. This is promoted by the desire to conform to physical attributes associated with conventional notions of beauty. For boys, parents and society tend to dump other baggage such as demanding physical strength, discouraging the expression of emotions, and promoting competitiveness. Their self-worth is often tied to sports achievements and career success, although most children carry this type of baggage.

Unintentionally, parents try to raise human *doings* rather than human *beings*. Inadvertently, children learn that their worth and entitlement are tied to what they "do" and how they look rather than who they are. Navigating through life with feelings of self-doubt is like climbing Mount Everest with a boulder on your back. This heavy weight makes every endeavor so much more difficult.

It is time for children to learn that repetitive, deeply-held ideas and beliefs are merely illusions imposed on them during their childhood. Unfortunately, these constructs can pervade throughout a person's entire life. These made-up notions feel so real that they become part of a person's soul, somewhat like a second skin. Shedding these ideas, and the thought patterns associated with them, is scary for many people, despite the fact that joy and freedom abound once they are released.

It can seem unimaginable that thoughts are not objectively real. Once a person has done the hard work of creating distance between their thoughts and their sense of self, and between their thoughts and their actions, the door to liberation opens.

This proverbial second skin can be shed when a person is willing to create a "third eye." This is essentially a new lens through which to observe that their thoughts are impermanent and fleeting. It allows a more neutral and objective view of the self, and of one's behaviors.

Thoughts seem so real, but they are not. Once a person realizes this, and learns to pause and focus on their breath when a thought arises, that thought will eventually dissipate. This is where regular practice of meditation can help. By learning to focus on one's breath, the process of separating from one's thoughts can begin.

Think of the idea of a "train of thought" as nothing but a repetitive habit. The thinker gets to choose whether or not to get on the train by following their thought, or to leave the thought on the train and allow it to depart from the station, as they return to their breath.

This is similar to the process of learning to tolerate one's feelings as they arise. Thoughts and feelings are intertwined and often arise in tandem. Learning to see that neither are permanent, and that both can be tolerated and gently released, is the pathway to clearing up one's emotional landscape.

Ironically, growth usually occurs in the messiness and muck of life. Painful situations are often the portal for transformation, as hardship requires a person to find new ways to observe their thoughts and to cope with their feelings. The loss of a job, death of a loved one, illness, end of an important relationship, or a financial crisis are painful examples of life's challenges. They often lead people to wake up to these lessons of mindful living, and begin to observe their lives through a new and different lens. They can start to see their ego at play as they begin to recognize habitual patterns, search for the origins of those patterns in their childhood, and ultimately transform.

A Weighty Issue

Lynne, the mother of twin sixteen-year-old boys and a thirteen-year-old girl, is slender and attractive. Being thin is important to her. Her sons are athletic and agile, and while they consume enormous quantities of food, they are also thin and muscular. Her daughter, Jackie, inherited her mother's propensity for weight gain but not for discipline.

Lynne recalls how much of an issue her weight was for her as a child. Her parents consistently prodded her to eat less, exercise more, and lose weight. While her siblings were offered french fries, soda, and any treats they desired, she was not. This always frustrated her and made her feel that she was not as loved and accepted as her siblings. Lynne was determined not to impose these feelings onto Jackie.

During the winter break from school in February, the family visited Lynne's parents in Florida. Lynne took Jackie shopping and purchased several new pairs of jeans for her. Jackie was excited to wear her new clothes to school.

About one month later, Jackie asked her mom if they could go shopping again for new jeans. Lynne did not understand why Jackie needed more clothing since they had shopped recently. With tears in her eyes, Jackie confessed that all of her new jeans no longer fit her as she had gained ten pounds in the past month. Lynne had noticed that Jackie was gaining weight precipitously, but she never wanted to ask Jackie about her weight as she did not want to make an issue of it.

Lynne learned that Jackie had been given $20 by her grandmother during their recent visit to Florida and was told that she could buy whatever she wanted. Jackie took that money to school every day. Her favorite period of the day was lunch as she sat at a fun table with great friends.

Every day, Jackie bought three large cookies for only $0.50 each at the school cafeteria to share with her friends, although the other kids barely ate them which left them for Jackie to enjoy on her own. Also, at the end of most school days, there were clubs and teams holding bake sales with delicious and inexpensive homemade and store-bought treats for sale in the school lobby. Jackie indulged in these as well. Since all of these items were sold at very low cost, the $20 went a long way in indulging her sweet tooth.

Lynne was triggered by this news. She was angry at her own mother for having given Jackie the money. She was also angry with the school for selling these items at a reduced cost, particularly since childhood obesity was such a mainstream issue. Nonetheless, she realized that getting angry at her mother or attempting to blame the school district was pointless. She knew that her mother's intention was to be generous and that she would make little headway with the school district regarding this issue.

She was also frustrated because she had talked to Jackie extensively and repeatedly about good nutrition, and she thought her daughter was following her rules and eating only the food she was sending to school. While her instinct was to reprimand Jackie, she knew that this was not the way to effectuate change. This was a sensitive subject for Jackie, who was already jealous of her skinny brothers and mother.

After a quick conversation with her conscious parenting coach to debrief about her feelings surrounding this situation, Lynne was able to release her fears, and approach Jackie calmly and compassionately.

The first order of business was to defuse the situation. She thanked Jackie for being honest about her daily food purchases at school. She told her how brave she was, and she joked with Jackie about how mad she was that Jackie had not brought home some of the delicious treats to share with her.

Lynne told Jackie that she was beautiful at any weight and that nothing could change the way she felt about her. She also acknowledged to Jackie that avoiding those delicious treats is so hard. Lynne's ability to empathize with her daughter and to use humor to relieve the tension helped Jackie calm down and not feel judged.

Lynne had done online research about the brand of cookies sold at school and shared with Jackie how unhealthy they were due to their high fat and calorie content. It was helpful to Jackie to understand the facts about these foods.

Then she asked Jackie to make three important promises. The first was that she would not go on a diet. Lynne explained that diets are meant for adults with medical issues. As a healthy young teenager, she need not and should not diet regardless of what her friends may do or say. Next, she asked Jackie to promise to eat all of the food that her mother sent with her every day. Finally, she asked Jackie to promise to eat dessert every night. Jackie eagerly agreed to all of these conditions. Notice that none of the requests involved dieting or reduced food consumption.

Lynne then asked Jackie if she had any ideas as to how to handle all of the treats sold at school. They talked about how the cookies and afterschool treats would all still be sold and might continue to tempt her. Jackie explained that she now understood how she was hurting herself with these purchases and that she had not made good choices.

She told her mother that she had been thinking about this problem for a while and that she decided that she did not need to take any money to school. In fact, she reported to her mother that she had already removed the remaining change from her backpack and put it in her piggy bank. She felt that if she did not have money, even change, to buy extra food, she simply would not be able to do so.

Meanwhile, Lynne took Jackie shopping for a new pair of jeans in a larger size so that Jackie would be comfortable. Jackie did not gain any more weight. By the end of the school year four months later, Jackie had lost those extra ten pounds and was able to wear her new clothes again. She asked her mother if they could donate the new, larger pairs of jeans, and her mother happily agreed.

This vignette offers many lessons about how to respond consciously to a child's behavior when the parent is triggered. Reacting, yelling, reprimanding, shaming, or criticizing the child actually perpetuates the undesirable behavior. Lynne had co-created the eating problem that Jackie inherited. Now Lynne realized that if there was a chance of solving the problem, she must function as the antidote.

Being the antidote to a child's emotions is a critical skill of a mindful parent. Just as fire cannot be successfully fought with fire, a child's big feelings cannot be successfully contained where a parent also expresses big feelings.

Jackie was a mirror to Lynne's childhood weight issue, which is why Lynne was triggered by Jackie's weight gain. Once Lynne realized that her daughter needed to be treated with kindness and respect, rather than judgment and criticism, Lynne was able to rise above her own trigger and desire to react to help Jackie create more permanent solutions.

A blueprint for a conscious response by a parent includes the following options:

- **Pause, breathe, and remain silent.**
- **Recognize the internal triggers and sit with them without reacting.**
- **Acknowledge to the child the courage it took to confess and take responsibility.**
- **Empathize with the child's feelings of disappointment and shame.**
- **Validate those feelings as normal and acceptable.**
- **Avoid dismissing the child's feelings.**
- **Share a similar story from your childhood.**
- **Inject humor and playfulness into the situation.**
- **Go on a fact-finding mission so the child understands the consequences of their actions.**
- **Engage the child in creating solutions.**
- **Recognize that the most effective solutions might be counterintuitive.**

- **Focus on the process of changing the behavior rather than the outcome.**
- **Leave space for the child to create their own solutions.**
- **Congratulate the child for recognizing their error and course-correcting.**
- **Congratulate yourself for your mindful, non-reactive response.**

The way in which children mirror their parent's behavior can be direct, as with Jackie and Lynne, or it may be indirect or inverted. Sometimes a child behaves in ways that are directly contrary to the parent's patterns. This is another way that a child might try to awaken a parent.

Mirror, Mirror

Duarte is a bright, friendly, eight-year-old boy. His father, Jamal, has become increasingly concerned about selfish behavior that Duarte has been exhibiting lately. Duarte refuses to share his toys, and when there are two treats available, he grabs both. He would rather throw one in the garbage than give it to his friend. Jamal is an incredibly giving and selfless person and parent. He shares everything with Duarte. Jamal gives Duarte food from his plate at Duarte's request and is always purchasing new toys and games for him.

Jamal started to wonder whether his selfless behavior was actually causing Duarte to be more selfish. He started thinking a lot about his own traumatic childhood. He recalled especially hard times when he had to leave his homeland abruptly due to political changes. He and his brother were sent to boarding school when he was only eleven years old. During this tumultuous period in his life, his family did not have much money. He was unable to travel to visit his parents often and he could not buy books and clothing, which made him jealous of his classmates. He promised himself that when he became an adult, his children would not suffer in this way.

Ironically, the more selfless Jamal was, the more selfish Duarte became. This is because Duarte was subconsciously reacting to his father's trauma and the fact that his father had never fully processed his feelings surrounding the chaos and scarcity inherent in his own childhood. Duarte was acting as a mirror to his father's behavior. In doing so, he was his father's greatest teacher.

If there was any chance to get Duarte to change his selfish behavior, his father would have to face the trauma of his childhood, process the fear and sadness of his youth, and release his pain. In doing so, he would be free to choose when to be a selfless role model for Duarte, and when to be more selfish so as to model self-worth and entitlement. While it is counterintuitive, being more selfish would free Duarte to be more selfless and kind. Duarte was not a selfish child, but he was exhibiting selfish behaviors.

Soon Jamal stopped buying gifts and toys for Duarte as often, and he enjoyed his full portion of the family's bounty rather than giving Jamal food from his plate. Shortly thereafter, he observed that Duarte was much more willing to share his treats, toys, and games with his friends. **Where a parent clears up his own emotional landscape, they free their children to do the same.**

Even where the parent's behavior is defined as "good," such as Jamal's selflessness, it was actually damaging his child. Duarte was literally screaming for his father to awaken. Only after Duarte's behavior became unbearable, was Jamal willing to look within and ascertain how his past trauma was influencing his current behavior and his parenting. His child's untoward behavior served as his path to awakening.

The first task is always awareness, followed by detachment, surrender, and transcendence. Once parents learn these critical lessons, they can begin to teach their children how to detach from their impermanent and often damaging thoughts and patterns. Parents need to actively teach these lessons and role model them to their children.

NOTES

11 SELF-COMPASSION

- As I become a more conscious parent, am I willing to let myself off the hook for my mistakes?
- Am I willing to look inward with compassion, rather than with self-blame and regret for the past?
- Do I understand that I cannot begin to meet my child's needs until I meet my own?
- Do I realize that I need to have self-compassion so that I can model that behavior?
- Do I recognize that my children need me to release my self-blame so that they can release theirs?

Self-care is more than manicures and massages. While those services are part of the physical care that can feel good and support wellness, self-care should include nurturing one's spirit, releasing regret, maintaining boundaries, reducing stress and anxiety, and validating oneself. For the sake of their children, parents need to nurture themselves in these sacred and spiritual ways.

When a parent is in pain, they need to both reach out for help and to delve inward. They need to give themselves permission to be imperfect, as their children are watching all aspects of their behavior. If they allow themselves to be imperfect and to fail, then their children will live more fearlessly knowing that they too can be imperfect and can fail, and that they are still okay, worthy, and whole.

Women often feel the need to put themselves down by highlighting their imperfections in order to seem humble. However, humility does not require self-humiliation and the two should not be conflated. In fact, true inner self-confidence should never be confused with arrogance, which stems from insecurity. Arrogance does not masquerade as self-confidence. Children need to know that self-love and self-compassion are essential elements of their sense of self. Once those are achieved, they will be okay regardless of what comes their way.

Girl Power

> *A group of fifteen-year-old girlfriends were engaged in a girls' empowerment group. As they were talking before the session began, each described a body part they hated the most. When the group began, the leader decided to try to change the narrative, so she asked each of them to describe one body part they loved the most. The exercise startled them, but soon they were joyfully highlighting their finest physical attributes.*
>
> *Some spoke of their hair and nails, while others expressed that they were most grateful for their brain and spinal cord. Every girl's choice was honored. Then they were asked to engage in the same process regarding their personalities and abilities. It was the first time in a long time that these girls felt that they had permission to talk about themselves in a positive way, and it was liberating for all of them.*

Children should be taught that they can be humble and self-confident at the same time. Boys tend to feel freer than girls to own their favorable attributes and take pride in their accomplishments without feeling that they are boasting. Girls tend to put themselves down.

These conventional expectations are so deeply ingrained that when a group of fifteen-year-old girls at sleep-away camp were asked to spend one week refraining from making any comments, either negative or positive, about anyone's appearance, clothes, or bodies, including their own, they refused mostly because it felt like an impossible exercise. The goal was to see if they could avoid both complimenting their friends, and judging themselves negatively. They found it inconceivable not to obsess about their thighs or their hair, as well as not to argue with their friends about how fat or ugly they looked.

Curiously, adults intuitively know how to help a friend in need, but they often do not afford themselves the same luxury. Remember how understanding Chloe was, early on in *Coffee Break-Down*, when her friend spilled coffee on her report? Similarly, when someone experiences a crisis and begins to self-deprecate and blame, their friend intervenes with kindness and caring. Yet when that same friend experiences their own crisis, they are often unable to treat themselves or their children with that same level of care, respect, and kindness.

Parents need to be that friend to themselves, and to share the new language of self-worthiness and self-compassion with their children. Every crisis is here to teach us life's lessons.

It's Never Too Late...

You may recall in Cut From a Different Cloth, *Jody, the rebellious teenager, and her mother Adele, who had difficulty communicating with one another. When Adele realized what was going on with Jody beneath the surface, she had a great deal of remorse and guilt. Adele began to understand how she had co-created Jody's reality and how unable she had been to meet Jody's emotional or social needs during her tumultuous teenage years.*

Adele also realized that living with sadness, regret, and guilt over how she parented Jody did nothing to help the current situation for either the parent or the child. Adele decided to begin to meditate daily, study more about conscious living, and start becoming a more mindful parent to all of her adult children.

This was challenging work as it required Adele to assess her own behavior and attitudes. As Adele looked inward, she began to see the depth of the expectations she had foisted upon Jody and all of her children. She had

hoped that Jody would succeed in life, which in turn would reflect well on her as a parent.

In retrospect, she realized that she had placed so many onerous demands on Jody, including academic excellence and social status. While her other children were able to withstand the rigid social and educational constructs Adele demanded of them, and therefore they were able to be more compliant, Jody was both unable and unwilling to comply.

Adele realized that Jody's independent and authentic spirit was actually a great gift that she should honor. She and Jody began to have deeper conversations during which Adele expressed her remorse and asked Jody for forgiveness. She also learned to listen to Jody more deeply, without interruption, regardless of whether she agreed or disagreed with her, even where Jody expressed anger or disappointment in her mother. It was time for Jody to be heard without judgment, criticism, or interference.

It was also time for healing. Adele knew that self-compassion was essential to this process. Adele made a conscious choice to forgive herself and to release her guilt. Adele wrote a letter to Jody expressing both her remorse and her need to forgive herself, as she understood that she had done the best she could during those years. Now that she knew better, she could and would do better.

Adele told Jody that she hoped that by releasing herself from the chains of regret, guilt, and self-blame, Jody would do the same. However, implicit in this path of reconciliation through self-compassion was the understanding that Adele had to completely release her expectations of Jody. She would no longer harbor disappointment about Jody's life choices. Instead, she would accept and honor them.

Adele became willing to accept Jody exactly as she was, rejoicing in her independent spirit. Jody was now an adult whose job was to re-parent herself and to live her best life. Adele would be there to listen and to hold space for Jody's feelings without criticism, honoring her voice, her choices, and her time-frame. In order to do so successfully, first Adele needed to quiet her own voice which had always been full of judgment and criticism.

The key to this renewed relationship was compassion for one another, and for themselves. **Regret keeps people mired in the past, and anxiety keeps them stuck in the future. The moment was now, and it was time for acceptance and unconditional love through connection and compassion.**

The door to freedom, self-worth, and conscious living is often locked by the confines of self-deprecation and lack of self-worth. Just knowing that these constraints can be shed can be transformative. Resistance will inevitably arise and should be observed with curiosity, equanimity, and inquisitiveness.

The goal is to look inward, recognize the resistance, honor it, and allow it until it is ready to be released. This work requires each person to be present in the moment in whatever form it may take, knowing that whatever thoughts and feelings arise are impermanent and will pass.

NOTES

12 RESILIENCE

- Are my actions helping to build my child's muscle of resilience?
- Have I paused to assess my own reaction to my child's behavior before responding?
- Can I allow my child to build resilience by not interfering in their learning process?
- Am I willing to merely be the container for my child's emotions?
- Am I being a good role model for resilience during adversity?

Resilience is a muscle that can be developed and strengthened over time with patience and practice. It is not unlike building muscle strength in the gym which requires repetition and practice. While some people may be more naturally resilient in the face of adversity, many need to learn to exercise the muscle of resilience in order to strengthen it.

When a child has difficulty with social cues or math problems, a parent might engage a social coach or a math tutor. Similarly, a parent can mindfully support and teach a child to learn to handle adverse situations that will inevitably come their way. The expression "give a person a fish, and they eat for a day; teach a person to fish and they eat for a lifetime" is apropos when dealing with a child's ability to cope with external events.

Parents who seek to help build a child's resilience must accept the basic principles of this book - that pain is a portal for growth, and that parents have to raise themselves in order to mindfully raise their children. Every parent needs to get out of their child's way, thereby allowing the child to experience pain, within reason, based on their developmental age and stage. Only then will the child learn to tolerate their own feelings and to accept the consequences of their actions. In turn, this practice will help a child learn that the behavior of others, while frustrating, is essentially due to that person's own set of unconscious patterns and reactions.

The conscious parent holds space for their child in order to allow that child to experience all of their feelings, while purposefully not interfering to lessen the pain. Holding space to allow a child to sit in and with their feelings, without trying to change those feelings or to fix the external situation, is the mindful path that helps the child to develop self-confidence and resilience. This goes back to the practice addressed earlier of avoiding the often intense desire to advise, fix, rescue, and protect.

This is a simple idea in concept, since it merely requires the parent to be present with a child who is in pain. Nonetheless, despite its simplicity, it is one of the most challenging things a parent can do for their child. **Parents often have a hard time tolerating their children's pain because they have not learned to tolerate their own pain.** It is so challenging because it requires allowing a loved one to feel their feelings, usually labeled as "negative," without interruption or intervention.

By holding space for a child, the conscious parent acts as the container in which the child can pour out all of their emotions. Just as a person cannot drink a cup of tea without having the cup, a child cannot fully express and experience their feelings unless they are confident that their parent is willing to be the safe container for all of their feelings. **The quiet, loving embrace of a parent is a most powerful tool.**

It is hard for a parent not to intervene to try to lessen a child's pain because the parent instinctively wants to fix, rescue, and protect their child, and usually has the tools to be able to do so. The irony is that by intervening and trying to help the child, the parent is actually robbing the child of a meaningful chance to build and strengthen the muscle of resilience as they learn to cope with the feelings created by their behavior, and to cope with the circumstances that caused those feelings.

Only through repeated instances where a child is allowed to experience life events without interference can the muscle of resilience grow. While there may be certain situations where a parent should intervene to protect a child, knowing when to do so requires the parent to determine their own motivation before interfering. Where the child's physical or emotional safety is imperiled, then the parent should act to help and support the child.

For example, where a child is being bullied relentlessly or where the parent of a teen suspects drug use, the parent can and should intervene. This requires the parent to discern when there is a valuable lesson to be learned by the child without parental intervention, and when the child's physical or spiritual growth or safety is at risk.

Resilience is a critical life skill that can best be learned when the parent gets out of the child's way. Resilience is an outgrowth of emotional tolerance. While it can be painful for a parent to witness, allowing a child to experience their experience is the path to building resilience.

A resilient child is one who has a sense of self-worth, listens to their internal voice, trusts their intuition, and knows that they cannot and need not control the actions of others. This is also the child who instinctively understands that the other person is often projecting their own sense of lack and unworthiness onto them, and that they need not react or absorb anyone else's judgment.

Pain Is Gain

Remember Ashley, the 5th-grader who was excluded from the birthday party? From that painful experience, Ashley learned that she was resilient. She had experienced her pain in all its rawness and learned to accept the situation as it was. She also learned that her feelings were temporary.

Realizing that although rejection and exclusion are painful, she was determined not to allow them to crush her spirit or change the way she felt about herself. Her sense of self-worth was entirely separate from what other people thought and did, even when their actions impacted her directly.

When Ashley's birthday was nearing, she chose not to invite the other girl to her party. However, she also decided not to distribute the invitations during class at school because she did not want to hurt the feelings of those she was not inviting, including the girl who had excluded her.

Ashley had empathy for what it felt like to be excluded. As Dawn mailed Ashley's birthday party invitations, she secretly thanked the other child who had excluded Ashley from her party, as she was grateful that her daughter learned several invaluable lessons. This is a great reminder that pain is a perfect portal for growth.

Similarly, when Rosie was cyber-bullied as described earlier in *What Goes Around Comes Around*, it took her a while to release her feelings of pain and embarrassment. However, the process of doing so inevitably built resilience and strength of character.

While Ashley and Rosie's parents were triggered by these unpleasant events, they also knew that the only way to help their daughters grow from their pain was to allow them to take as much time as they needed to feel angry, frustrated, and embarrassed. They knew that it was neither helpful to try to erase or ease their raw and tender feelings, nor to try to intervene to fix these situations. Their parents shared stories about similar things that happened to them as children, although in the case of Rosie, the advent of the internet had provided the vehicle for bullying behavior.

No doubt Ashley and Rosie became more inured to the judgments of others and ultimately more self-confident as they learned that they could cope with the fallout of whatever arose in their lives without turning their pain inward and without feeling badly about themselves. They both grew to become resilient, mindful, and insightful adults. Rosie learned in later years that all of those three boys had struggled with the memory of how they had hurt her. They felt remorse and regret, and they too had to learn to forgive themselves.

NOTES

13 DETACHMENT

- **Am I willing to detach from my thoughts, fears, and desire for specific outcomes?**
- **Can I listen to my inner voice when parenting my child?**
- **Can I ignore societal norms and expectations when they do not serve my child?**
- **Can I meet my child's needs rather than my egoic desire for them to conform?**
- **Can I define success as what is best for my child?**
- **Am I meeting my child's needs at this present moment?**

Children are perfectly imperfect and flawlessly flawed. Acceptance of this truth requires detachment and neutrality. If the reader learns only one thing from these teachings, let it be that the manner in which a parent repeatedly reacts to their child will have an indelible impact on how the child sees themselves. A parent's reaction to their child's achievements or failures matters more than what the child actually did or did not achieve. This is the essence of detachment from outcomes.

What is the answer for parents who struggle with troubling behaviors in their children? The answer always lies within the parents. **Ironically,**

if a parent wants a particular behavior to stop, in order to get it to stop, they should stop wanting it to stop. Instead, acceptance is key, and this includes acceptance of oneself and of the child exactly as they are. Only through acceptance, coupled with awareness, curiosity, and detachment, does the chance for real change arise.

Why does a child misbehave? One reason is that they have an underlying unmet emotional and/or physical need. The parent dealing with a child who repeatedly misbehaves should detach from their own frustration, anger, and worry before acting. The parent who is in a more neutral state of mind can identify the child's needs and try to meet them.

Children are attuned to their parent's energy. They pick up on their parent's underlying fear and disappointment even more than they do on their parent's words. A child knows when their parent is disappointed in them. The energy in the home may inadvertently be perpetuating the child's resistance and untoward behavioral patterns. Parents who are willing to take responsibility for their actions and reactions, without self-blame, will raise their awareness and recognize that this new vision offers an opportunity for change.

The parent's anxiety might rise each time the child repeats an upsetting behavior. This parent should sit with those feelings and observe them without trying to stop them or distract themselves. Eventually those uncomfortable feelings, once processed, will dissipate. The parent needs to learn to ride the waves of their emotions without reacting, trusting that their feelings are temporary and will subside. This is the essence of detachment and it is the path to helping shift behaviors in the child.

Parents often say that detachment feels impossible because they love their children so deeply and therefore they want so much for them. **This is the trap - where need is disguised as love. Wanting anything for anyone else is nothing but ego.**

In order to overcome this need, parents would be wise to parent their own children as though they were someone else's children. Parents often find that when a friend or relative's child has a problem, it is so much easier to be able to give more mindful, detached, loving advice than when their own child encounters the same problem. For example, when another parent confides that their child got a poor grade on a test, it seems easy and intuitive to suggest that it is no big deal, that it is merely one test score, and just to let it go. This provides proof that parents get much too enmeshed with their own child's performance causing them to react mindlessly because they are triggered. This is why detachment from outcomes, and release of agendas, are crucial to the mindful parenting paradigm.

Detachment is an art which has to be cultivated. Without detachment from outcomes, and without a neutral approach to our children which is not charged with our own egoic desires, the "misery-go-round" continues. **Allowing children to experience their experiences, without intervention, interference, or drama, is the path to teaching resilience through detachment.**

Occasionally, a teachable moment will arise when the parent can gently intervene and guide a child toward a behavioral shift. This will occur when the child trusts that their parent has no hidden agenda or expectation, when they intuitively understand that their parent is merely trying to teach an important lesson, and when they know that their parent is not attached to whether the lesson is actually learned.

The parent must be completely neutral and non-reactive when explaining to the child another way to view a particular situation, without any investment in whether the lesson is actually learned. Until such a moment arrives and the parent discerns that the child is open to a new way of seeing something, there is nothing to be done except to accept, connect, and show unconditional love. **Conscious parenting is about raising the parents. After all, it is called "parenting," not "childing."**

The Art of Letting Go

> Remember Joey, who continually craved the attention of his father Scott after he returned from work each night? Joey often likes to roughhouse as

he seeks his father's undivided attention. Joey's mother finds herself triggered by his behavior. As with any behavior, before assessing whether Joey needed to be stopped or restrained at any given moment, it was important for his mother to assess her conditioned ideas surrounding this type of physical play.

For example, she needed to ask herself whether it was truly disrespectful behavior or whether her cultural conditioning was affecting the way she perceived it. It was joyful for Joey to play with his father this way as he missed him during the day, especially on those days when Scott had been on call and could not return home before Joey's bedtime.

Joey's mother realized that she needed to neutralize her response and remove herself. It was up to Scott to determine the level of play he would allow and to just have fun playing with Joey. This made Joey feel even more important to his dad. Joey's need for his father's attention trumped his mother's need to control their interactions.

Applying Consciousness

A mother was in a panic as her daughter, Wendy, a high-school senior, had not yet received a college acceptance, whereas many of her peers had. Wendy selected her first-choice school, although neither she nor her mother could articulate a clear reason why they preferred this school, except that several of her friends wanted to attend it. When the rejection from that school arrived, Wendy was miserable and disappointed. She took the rejection personally. Her mother's reaction was even more severe, and they both cried and panicked for days.

Both Wendy and her mother were unable to see the beauty in this rejection or the lesson of detachment. For more than a month, Wendy's mother remained anxious and sad. In doing so, she felt she was showing her daughter how much she cared about her and about her success.

Instead, her mother's overreaction signaled to Wendy her lack of confidence that she would get accepted into any college. It made the rejection seem so much worse to Wendy and signaled her mother's fear about her future. Also, Wendy and her mother bought into the illusory belief that Wendy's first-choice college was the only school in which Wendy would find happiness.

This is a great example of how attachment to an artificial outcome can be damaging in many ways. It sends unconscious messages to the child that they are not good enough, that they will not find happiness unless they achieve a particular outcome over which they have no control, and that the outcome matters more than the process, even where the outcome is arbitrary.

Wendy also felt a great sense of shame and sadness that she had disappointed her mother. All of these feelings could have been lessened if she had been given the message that this rejection would serve her in the long run, even if she could not yet see how that might occur. This rejection was not a judgment on her abilities and background, since there are so many unknown factors that go into these determinations. This was simply a decision by an anonymous admissions committee that this was not the right school for Wendy.

Had her mother been more neutral about this rejection, rather than overreacting dramatically, Wendy could have learned to accept it and in turn, she would have been happier for her friends who were accepted, trusting that she too would find her way and end up just where she belonged. A parent's reaction to an external situation in the child's life inevitably informs and guides a child's emotional reaction. **When parents learn to trust the universe, their children follow suit.**

NOTES

14 DISCERN AND ATTUNE

- Can I drown out the outside noise and focus on my child?
- Am I able to discern when my child needs me to be silent and listen?
- Am I also able to discern when my child needs me to intervene for their safety and well-being?
- Do I have the courage to let my child's authentic voice be heard?
- Can I attune to my family's values rather than societal convention?

When a parent recognizes that their child is perfectly imperfect and flawlessly flawed, they accept the child as they are and revel not just in their accomplishments and gifts, but also in their weaknesses and ordinariness.

A child whose temperament, interests, and abilities differ from those of the parent can present a unique challenge for a parent who may feel disappointed that they did not create a "mini-me." It is important for the parent to recognize their feelings of disappointment, but this same parent also needs to shift to a state of abundance by recognizing that each child has unique gifts, abilities, and passions that can and should be valued.

Unconditional acceptance of the child's innate personality, weaknesses, and strengths is one of the greatest gifts that a parent can bestow on their child. This is also the path to allowing that parent to discern and attune to the needs of their particular child. What works with one child may not be effective with a sibling or friend.

Only through unconditional acceptance, coupled with discernment and attunement, can a parent tune in to that child's needs in order to guide and support them effectively. Discernment allows the parent to tune into their child's particular needs and to distinguish them from those of their other children, as they can vary from child to child.

Stage Fright

Safia, a thirteen-year-old 7th-grader, was thrilled to get the lead role in the school play. After months of rehearsals, it was time for opening night and Safia's heart was beating fast. When the curtain opened, suddenly fear overtook her, and she forgot her first few lines. She stood on stage speechless and silent. After a few moments, she regrouped, and the rest of the play went smoothly.

After the performance, Safia could not help but focus on those first few moments. She became stuck on the fact that she had messed up and she was terribly embarrassed. Her friends tried to cheer her up by telling her she did great and that they hardly noticed her mistakes, which only made her feel worse because she knew they were obvious.

Safia's mindful parents took a different path. Instead of trying to distract her from her feelings around this small mess up, or to dissuade her by saying things like "it was not so bad," "no one noticed," and "you'll do better in tomorrow's performance," they discerned that she needed to experience her feelings without distraction or resistance.

They reflected back all of the uncomfortable feelings she was having by saying things like, "I see that you are embarrassed about missing your first few lines" and "that must have been rough on you." Her mother recounted a time when she was in a cheerleading troupe and missed some steps, causing the whole group to be off the beat in front of a large crowd. She recalled how embarrassed and upset she had felt, and she told Safia that she could relate to her feelings. Her father mentioned that he missed an easy soccer goal in a final game, causing his team to lose.

By allowing their daughter to experience her emotions and by being the container for the full expression of them, rather than trying to avoid or deny them, this budding actress soon metabolized her disappointment and let it go. The next night Safia was on her game and remembered all of her lines.

The developmental age of the child must be considered when discerning how to respond to any situation. For example, when a four-year-old was in a choir performance and forgot the words to a song, she was tearful. Her father realized that at her young age she needed to be supported in a different way as mere reflection and containment were above her level of comprehension.

Unlike Safia, this very young child needed to be told that her performance was fine, and that it was okay that she forgot the words to the song. Her father also told her that he was so happy to attend her singing performance and that he was proud to see her on the stage. He let her cry until she eventually calmed down.

Under either circumstance, it is often best to refrain from saying things like "no one noticed your mistake" or "your performance was perfect." These comments ignore the reality that the child did not perform as well as they would have liked, which in turn deprives them of the opportunity to experience the natural emotional fallout of their mistake. It is usually better for parents to allow a child to experience their experience and the resulting consequences and feelings of disappointment, and to let them know that they trust that they will be okay.

Either approach requires discernment by the parent as to when and how to intervene, and when to step back. The parent needs to consider multiple factors including the age of the child, the child's developmental stage (which can be different from their biological age), the child's temperament, and the circumstances. With older children, it is often better to allow them to experience their feelings without intervention and to hold space for them.

Discerning what approach to take when raising a child who struggles to achieve or who is unmotivated is more challenging. When a child is consistently underachieving, it usually is a signal to the parent that they must figure out what is occurring beneath the surface of their child's lack of achievement. There could be a myriad of reasons for poor performance, from a processing disorder to social struggles.

Connection and attunement to the child help the parent understand the etiology of under-performance. In addressing academics specifically, start by ascertaining if there is a particular subject in which the child is struggling regularly or whether there has been a recent change in the child's overall performance.

This is where grades can offer insight. Grades provide information to the parent about how the child is doing at a particular moment in time. Sadly, grades are often mistaken as symbols of the child's worth and abilities, which trigger the parent's ego. The parent should recognize that grades are only a single measure of how a child is performing and whether they grasp the material.

There should be no pressure on the child to achieve high grades. This requires the parent to detach from the reflective glory often associated with high achievement. Neither honor roll nor dean's list measure a child's worth. Instead, when a child does not achieve a satisfactory grade, ask the child whether they like the subject or the teacher, whether they are having difficulties with classmates, whether they are having trouble with comprehension, or whether something else is upsetting them. The approach differs when a child is not doing well in most subjects, compared to a child who is struggling in one particular subject.

Once the parent determines whether the problem stems from disorganization, an organic issue, difficulty with comprehension, emotional concerns, or social struggles, the parent can take appropriate action. Where the parent has detached from their egoic connection to their child's achievement, they can begin to figure out what the child really needs.

There are many ways to get help for a child. Tutoring either in a particular subject or in organizational skills can be helpful. However, if a child consistently requires tutoring in a particular academic subject, the parent should consider whether the child is being asked to perform above their ability. While parents often want their children to be enrolled in honors and advanced-level curricula, this does not always serve the child's best interests. The parent should recognize that a child is unlikely to excel in every subject, and that is okay.

Being attuned to the particular child will help the parent discern when to push that child and when to back off. If the parent knows that their child is usually hesitant to try a new sport or activity but often ends up liking it, the child may need to be gently prodded. This does not mean that they should be offered rewards for their participation, but they should be strongly encouraged to try the activity.

If the child is shy and has difficulty in new situations, the parent might try to figure out strategies to make them more comfortable, such as having a friend join them or offering to stay nearby. Also, consider that the child might be shy because they feel they are being judged. They may fear that they will not live up to expectations and may be embarrassed. The parent will not know this unless they listen deeply to the child's concerns.

Parents are often surprised when they see that quiet attunement allows their children to create their own solutions. Figuring out the reasons underlying the child's attitude, feelings, and reactions is essential to creating solutions.

Whatever the parent chooses to do, they should not be persuaded by what other parents or children are doing. If your child is adamant that they do not want to attend sleep-away camp even though most of their friends are doing so, perhaps it is best not to force the situation. Have a frank conversation about why they are hesitant and discern the source of their reluctance.

Give the child agency and power over some decisions, particularly those that are non-essential to their health, education, and overall well-being. While every child must attend some type of grade school, summer camp is not a legal requirement so every effort should be made to honor the child's feelings while trying to ascertain the source of their fears and worries.

Whenever possible, the child's choices should be honored. Where the child's choices could not be honored, where a promise was not kept, or where the parent realizes that they have made an error in whatever choices they made, the parent should be transparent and apologize to their child.

To Err is Human, to Apologize Is Mindful

> *Nancy, a sweet, loving four-year-old girl adores her father Nicolas. He is a hard-working entrepreneur who works long hours but makes sure to make time for his beloved daughter. He often schedules business meetings after her bedtime so he can be present to put her to bed. Nancy and Nicolas share many special routines, one of which is that he always tucks her into her bed and kisses her goodnight.*
>
> *One night, Nicolas was on a business call in his home office. The call lasted longer than he expected. As he continued to talk on his mobile phone, he gathered up his things for his next meeting and left the house forgetting to say goodnight to Nancy. About fifteen minutes later, when he was not near his home, his wife called asking where he was. She explained that Nancy was hysterical as she went to her father's office and found that he had left the house before tucking her in and kissing her goodnight.*
>
> *Nicolas spoke with Nancy on the phone, apologizing profusely for forgetting to say goodnight. He tried to explain that he had gotten distracted by a call which had continued for longer than expected. He promised to make it up to her, and planned to pick her up from school the next two days and take her for a special treat.*
>
> *Nancy was inconsolable as her father's explanations did not soothe her, although eventually she finally fell asleep. The following morning she was still upset and she reiterated to her father how disappointed and sad she was feeling about his oversight. He apologized to her again, expressing his authentic remorse, but he also allowed her to express her feelings of sadness to him as he remained calm and present with her. Nicolas kept his promise and picked Nancy up from school that day.*

They had a wonderful afternoon together and Nancy was able to release her sadness.

Nicolas felt terrible about his oversight. However, he forgave himself as he also knew that this incident was a great opportunity for both of their growth as there were many lessons to be learned from it. **Growth often occurs at the extremes in life, either in times of pain or joy.**

In deconstructing this event, there were wonderful lessons for both Nancy and Nicolas: Nicolas had the chance to see first-hand the depth and intensity of the incredible bond he shares with Nancy. While he always knew it, it was priceless for him to observe. Nancy got to see that her father is human and fallible. Nicolas did one of the most powerful things that a parent can do, which is to apologize to their child. Nicolas taught Nancy the essential lesson that when she makes a mistake, she should have the humility to recognize her error and apologize.

Nicolas allowed Nancy to be sad. He did not try to stop her, and he did not reprimand her for her intense reaction. This taught Nancy that she can be upset with her father, that she is free to express herself, and that she can recover from it. Her sadness was real and deep, but it was also temporary like a wave in the ocean. Her feelings were honored and processed without fear or anger.

While Nicolas initially felt terrible for his oversight, ultimately he was able to let himself off the hook and honor his own fallibility. Also, because Nicolas had compassion for himself, he taught Nancy to have self-compassion, which would bolster her self-esteem and serve her well. **Pain is inevitable in all of our lives, and if endured mindfully, without reactivity or resistance, it can teach many lessons.** This incident provided the perfect lesson for conscious living.

Inherent in the parent's willingness to hear a child's authentic voice and to accept that a child must learn to endure pain, is a parent's willingness to honor an essential boundary by not always conforming to social convention even if it may affect the child's social standing. Children want and need to fit in, especially during their formative years. Therefore, parents should weigh the importance of allowing their child to be one of the gang against the family's personal needs and values.

Family Values

> *Nicoletta, a twelve-year-old girl, was new to her middle school and was trying desperately to fit in. She wanted to be accepted into the popular group and even changed her schedule so that she could sit at the cool lunch table. One day early in the school year, several of the girls at her table were talking about a dance class they were taking together. Nicoletta got the details and decided that joining this class would be a way to connect with these girls outside of school.*
>
> *Upon returning home that day, Nicoletta excitedly asked her mother to sign her up, not realizing that the time conflicted with the religious school program in which she was enrolled with her cousins. Nicoletta pleaded with both parents to allow her to skip religious school this year so she could take the dance class. They thought about it but decided that attending this religious school program with her cousins was an*

important family value. This was an essential boundary that they were not willing to cross.

Both parents empathized with Nicoletta's desire to attend this particular dance class and her disappointment that she was not able to do so. It was important to them that she receives a religious education, that she sees her cousins weekly, and that she learns the important lesson that at times she cannot have her way.

Nicoletta remained angry for a long time but eventually she came to terms with her parents' decision and accepted it. There were other opportunities to socialize with these girls outside of school, and her parents made extra efforts to make sure she did so.

Nicoletta's parents had to discern what really mattered to their family regardless of what social convention or status might have called for. They were sorry to disappoint her by refusing to enroll her in this dance class, but they agreed that this would teach her important lessons. She would learn that there are times when following the crowd is not necessary or possible, and that enhancing her social status was not the most important goal to which she should aspire. In the same vein, they did not always purchase the latest fad or fashion for her until they had discerned whether it was within their budget, whether she really liked it, and whether it was appropriate. **Pain is one of the most poignant and powerful portals for growth and transformation.**

NOTES

15 AUTHENTICITY AND ABUNDANCE

- Have I communicated to my child that they are worthy?
- Is my love for my child unconditional or is it based on external measures?
- Have I been a role model for living in the present moment without worry or regret?
- Am I willing to apologize when I get it wrong and to course-correct?
- Does my family swim in the sea of abundance or the ocean of lack?

A child who is parented mindfully will attune themselves inwardly and develop a strong sense of self-worth and self-confidence. It is through this inner attunement that their authentic spirit and voice will be fully expressed. It is through this parenting paradigm that a child will thrive.

This is the child who will intuitively know that they do not need to conform to social norms, to meet others' agendas, or to get approval from external sources to feel worthy and whole. This is the child who knows that they are enough regardless of their achievements. This is the child who will have a high vibrational field and will attract things that meet that vibration.

Such a child is most likely to find their highest trajectory in life and to manifest abundance. They will have an inner sense of value detached from what others think. They will know that they can flow with life and tolerate all that they may encounter.

Abundance is most likely to flourish in an environment of authentic, unconditional love. Not based on any single transaction, experience, or encounter, the ability to swim in the sea of abundance is linked to a lifetime of conscious living. Abundance can be manifested through detachment, non-resistance, connection, and boundaries.

Raising a child is not unlike tilling the soil for a bountiful harvest. A farmer knows not to expect a good harvest unless the soil has been prepared with the right nutrients, sunlight, and consistent care over time. **Each moment-to-moment interaction with a child affords yet another opportunity to water the field and till the soil, allowing for the plant's healthy growth.**

When the parent gets it wrong and reacts mindlessly, they should be gentle on themselves as they accept that getting hooked into mindless reactions and patterns is going to happen on occasion. Such moments offer an opportunity to course-correct and apologize, which then provides more nutrients for more growth.

There is great power in the parent's willingness to apologize and show true remorse to a child when they have veered off course. **Vulnerability is a show of great strength.** The messages to the child are that everyone is fallible, and that expressing remorse is a sign of one's humanity and humility. This is also a great way for the parent to role model the values of empathy, respect, and kindness.

The parent then needs to find their way back by course-correcting through more conscious approaches. Self-compassion is a key to moving forward as a parent who becomes mired in self-deprecation will remain stuck. Self-compassion also teaches the child that not only are mistakes inevitable, but that they need not sabotage growth. When a parent changes direction, they teach their child to be flexible and not to get stuck in their ego. This offers a great role model for healthy, joyful living.

An Anxious Legacy

> Rodrigo, the parent of sixteen-year-old Tommy, did not realize how nervous he always was, and how he did not trust himself. He would check to see that he had his keys several times after leaving his house or locking his car, and he incessantly worried that he left the stove on or the house unlocked.
>
> Rodrigo was not even aware of his own habits until one day when he began to notice how anxious Tommy had become. He saw that Tommy would check his backpack several times before leaving the house to make sure he had his homework, his lunch, and all of his belongings. He observed that Tommy would check the door repeatedly to make sure that it was locked even after he had already confirmed it.
>
> At first, Rodrigo did not understand how Tommy had become so anxious. Then he started thinking back on his own childhood and realized that his own mother exhibited similar traits, although they were expressed in other ways. He recalled that she refused to use a public restroom or to walk on the floor of a hotel room barefoot. He recalled that she also repeatedly checked that she had all of her personal belongings.

Rodrigo realized that he had inadvertently inherited these worries from his mother, and without realizing it, he had passed them down to his son. Naturally, his mother never suggested to Rodrigo that he should do these things, nor did Rodrigo suggest this behavior to Tommy. Rather, this happened through the process of osmosis, as he and in turn his son were simply observing their respective parents and taking it all in.

Rodrigo set out to change this pattern, first by talking to Tommy about what he had observed and then by making a determined effort to stop worrying and start trusting himself. This became an inside joke between Rodrigo and Tommy whenever either of them would second-guess themselves and repeat any of these habitual behaviors. They joked that Tommy's homework could not magically jump out of his backpack.

Both of them found that they did not need to live in such a worried state and eventually they stopped repeating these mindless behaviors. They had both become stuck in this mindset until Rodrigo, the parent, became aware of it, was willing to examine its origins, and worked on shifting the pattern. It was only through awareness that change could occur.

Many parents believe that worrying about their children is inevitable. In fact, many parents ascribe to the notion that a parent who worries incessantly about their children truly loves them. **The beliefs that worry equates with love, and that the more the child is loved the more the parent worries, are simply untrue. It is possible to love deeply without worry.**

Some parents, if responding honestly, might also acknowledge the belief that if they worry enough, bad things will not happen to them or their children. This is another illusion that keeps parents stuck and is entirely false.

Worry is rooted in fear of future events that have not yet occurred and may never occur. Worrying about the future causes anxiety, which can inadvertently be passed down to a child. Anxiety is an insidious, albeit entirely made-up, thought process that can impact every aspect of a person's life and can be exhausting. In reality, worry has nothing to do with love. Similarly, regret stems from disappointment over past incidents and behavior which can lead to shame and self-blame.

Both of these mindsets - worry and regret - are rooted in feelings of lack and scarcity that can keep parents, and in turn their children, stuck and miserable. Focusing on the present moment, free from regret about the past or worry about the future, allows abundance and flow to manifest. **Abundance is the sense that life is full and good exactly as it is.** Flow is the ability to accept whatever comes your way, knowing that there are lessons to be learned. It allows a person to become immersed in the present moment without being burdened by past regrets or future worries. **The key is to remember that it is always NOW, as past and future are imaginary, existing only in the mind.**

Sadly, most parents spend their lives swimming against the current in the ocean of lack, which can present as worry, jealousy, or competitiveness. Parents can easily get stuck in this ocean as it is well-known and familiar, but it is easy to drown there. At the same time, it can be terrifying to reach the shore and start to choose to swim in the sea of abundance, and many are too scared to even try. At best, they tread water, never finding their footing.

The sea of abundance offers joy and flow as it is rooted neither in the past nor the future, but in this present moment. Abundance is free from feelings of worry, jealousy, comparison to others, or competitiveness. It is the space where trust endures as the parent knows that things will unfold exactly as they are meant to in order for lessons to be learned and for life to be lived fully and joyfully.

The parent who resides in a mindset of abundance knows that life is not a zero-sum game. They also know and trust that they cannot, and need not control external events. Instead, they trust that their child has the skills to handle life's uncertainties, while understanding that each life event offers bountiful lessons.

Those with a greater sense of self-worth tend to swim more consistently in the sea of abundance with less fear. They know when they have mindlessly regressed and dipped their toes into the ocean of lack. Through the skills they have learned in mindful parenting and living, these parents are able to shift their mindset without drama. This, in turn, allows them to support and guide their children with greater ease and confidence.

Without raising their awareness, parents can stay stuck in a mindset of scarcity for an entire lifetime, swimming upstream against the current, often feeling lost in the undertow with no way out. They feel victimized when they or their children do not manifest good things in their lives, and they tend to blame others and even fate for their or their children's misfortune. **Those who are willing to awaken recognize that their approach to life is a choice they make, trusting that living with authenticity and abundance is the pathway to finding joy, meaning, and purpose.**

NOTES

16   OPTIONS: ACCEPT, LEAVE, OR CHANGE

- In any given situation, do I realize that there are only three options - accept, leave, or change?
- Have I accepted that I cannot change anyone but myself?
- Am I willing to cede control over other people and external events?
- Once I have decided whether to accept or leave, can I do so with equanimity?
- Can I avoid creating drama and just act?

There are only three options from which to choose in life in any given moment or circumstance: *accept, leave, or change,* with the caveat that a person can only change themselves. The idea that someone can change another person is mired in the illusion that a person has a measure of control over another. The only person that anyone can truly change is themselves. Therefore, to accept or to leave are essentially the choices one has in life, while always striving to awaken, transform, and change ourselves.

With children there is no turning back. Unlike every other relationship in life which affords an avenue to exit, such as friendship, work, and marriage, loving parents will neither leave their children nor can they change them. This leaves the single option of acceptance; and acceptance will ultimately serve the child's greatest growth and sense of self.

Acceptance of the child's essence in all their glory and with all their flaws is essential to mindful parenting. Every child seeks to be honored for their strengths as well as their weaknesses. Sadly, the parent who never felt deeply accepted and appreciated for their own authentic spirit often conveys this to the child who inherits a painful legacy.

The chain can only be broken when the parent chooses to awaken and become enlightened to a more conscious and mindful approach. This requires listening to the child to ascertain their authentic choices, spirit, and voice, letting their child know that they are accepted and loved unconditionally, exactly as they are. Only this approach will convey to the child that they are worthy and good enough.

To trust that one is good enough is the answer to the most crucial questions in life:

Do you hear me? Am I worthy?

The Art of Acceptance

Tamar and Ari are the parents of a fourteen-year-old daughter, Shoshana, an 8th-grader. Throughout the past five years, Shoshana had been having trouble making and sustaining friendships. While she had been beloved in her younger years, as she and her peers got older and more sophisticated, Shoshana's friends started to reject her. At times, they would whisper and giggle while pointing at her. Her feelings were deeply hurt and her self-esteem was imploding.

As they noticed this shift over time, Tamar and Ari became distraught. They were aware that she was socially awkward, was missing social cues, and was acting childishly. When either of them observed Shoshana behaving awkwardly in a social situation, afterward they admonished her for doing so, and questioned her about the foolish choices she was making. They also blamed her for losing friends. This behavior was triggering a lot of fear in them.

Tamar and Ari noticed that families within their social circle were getting together but that their family was often being excluded, which they attributed to the fact that their friends' children did not want to socialize with Shoshana. Finally, they sought the help of a social coach for Shoshana, as well as a mindful parenting coach for themselves. They realized that they had started to favor their younger son, who behaved in more socially acceptable ways and had more friends. Their coach highlighted their fears around Shoshana's losing friends and their anger that their entire family was being excluded.

They began to learn that it was their job to honor Shoshana's voice exactly as it was. They knew that Shoshana has many wonderful *qualities as she is artistic, studious, funny, and kind. While they could support her growth through social coaching, role modeling, and role-playing, the most important thing that they could do for her was to love her unconditionally exactly as she was.*

They learned that Shoshana's sense of self-worth would be more determined by how they responded to her than by whether her peers accepted or rejected her. They also knew that by refusing to accept Shoshana as she was, they were wounding her spirit further.

Their coach suggested that they take back the proverbial streets by no longer allowing other teenagers or even their own friends to determine how they felt. Their daughter was fabulous and they adored her. If she could not find her tribe in her middle or high school years, perhaps she would do so later in life. They realized that their focus on having friends and being popular in their community was not serving their family, and became secondary to their child's best-interests.

While Shoshana still experienced sadness when she was excluded, she found a few friends who understood and appreciated her. Moreover, she learned that friends are not the most important people in her life, and that they come and go. She had a loving, understanding, and accepting family. This sea-change in perspective of her family had an enormous impact on how she saw herself.

As Shoshana started to feel better about herself, she felt more relaxed and became less dependent upon approval from peers for her happiness. In turn, her grades improved. Also, as she became less stressed and as she matured over the next few years, her social anxiety and awkwardness diminished. The family was able to make light of the situation and found great joy in being together. Their happiness was no longer tethered to whether they or their children were liked and accepted by others. It was truly a liberating experience.

Tamar and Ari learned invaluable lessons which they were able to pass on to their children. They learned that they could accept or leave any situation. They also learned that they could not control the reactions of others, nor could they make other kids like their child, but that no longer mattered.

If their child was having difficulty sustaining friendships, then those friendships just did not matter. Learning these lessons was priceless as the family got to choose to experience their lives through the lens of abundance, and to choose with whom they did or did not socialize. This experience also helped them to discern that their truly close friends were those who did not exclude their family during hard times.

NOTES

17 POWER AND RESPONSIBILITY

- Have I been a role model for self-worth?
- Have I instilled the values of gratitude and humility?
- Do I avoid self-deprecation, recognizing that humiliation is not humility?
- Have I taught my child that profound self-acceptance also means the courage to act?

Gratitude is an outgrowth of mindful living. Children who are raised in a conscious way inevitably feel worthy and are consequently grateful, while also being humble. This practice requires unconditional acceptance, connection, as well as the imposition of clear boundaries.

The parent who cannot say "no" to their child may think that they are expressing love or may even fear that they will lose their child's love by denying their requests, but actually the parent who reinforces boundaries provides a sense of safety and limits. **Limits inherently inculcate gratitude, which is more loving than any purchase could be.**

The parent who refuses to purchase a new dress for every party to which their teenage daughter is invited, teaches their child that life is bountiful regardless of how many dresses she owns. The parent who honors their son's love of baseball by taking them on a countrywide tour of baseball stadiums offers meaningful experiences that are more important and memorable than any purchase possibly could be.

The sixteen-year-old who gets a new car the moment they obtain their driver's permit merely because all their friends in the neighborhood did so is not learning essential lessons and is unlikely to be grateful. These are just examples of how a child's spirit can best be honored through love and limits.

A parent's self-talk is equally important in imbuing self-esteem in their children. The slender mother who repeatedly complains about being unable to lose the last five pounds is teaching her children that their self-worth is tied to their weight, and inadvertently sends the message that humiliation is the path to humility. Instead, that mother could express gratitude for her healthy body while being a role model for good eating habits.

A parent can also be a role model for gratitude by expressing their thanks for the bounty in her life as this teaches gratitude to their children. The parent who is grateful for their creative child who is not great at math, or for their little engineer who cannot play an instrument, teaches that worthiness is not based on specific external measures.

A self-confident child likely has a parent who feels good about themselves. A parent's sense of self-worth is not to be mistaken for arrogance. Rather, it is actually the opposite. **Self-worth leads to humility and gratitude, which derive from an inner knowing that one can tolerate all that life throws one's way with equanimity.**

Teaching this to children will help them to develop skills that allow them to tolerate the spectrum of external events that occur in life. They will learn by example how to handle their emotions, while taking action with clarity and without reactivity or resistance to the "as is."

Self-deprecation does not teach worthiness. Humiliation should not be equated with humility. A child who is taught that their essence is divine feels deeply connected to themselves and to the world.

Teach a child that they have a responsibility to the world, but that their first responsibility is to themselves, and that they are whole just as they are. Consequently, they will want to save and protect the world because they feel a great sense of power and responsibility.

Acceptance Breeds Success

Remember Shoshana from the Art of Acceptance? *She was accepted into a top college where she studied business and screenwriting. She later earned a Ph.D. and went on to teach at a prestigious university where she also co-wrote a movie with her husband. The movie was accepted into a well-known film festival. She earned accolades and enormous wealth of every kind.*

These lessons may manifest in an infinite number of ways, and sometimes the payoff is delayed as it was for Shoshana. Nonetheless, the child who navigates life with the inner knowledge of their self-worth will inevitably choose exactly the path that life calls for in any given moment.

Every child may zig-zag in life as there is neither a straight line toward success nor a single definition of it. In fact, success is not a destination, but a momentary understanding that life is unfolding exactly as it is meant to. The goal of mindful parenting is to teach children to surrender to life's unfolding while taking action to chart their unique divine course.

NOTES

18 EMOTIONAL FREEDOM THROUGH CONSCIOUS LIVING

- Have I had the courage to witness my fears and act anyway?
- Has my child seen that I have charted my own course regardless of what others think?
- Have I taught my child that it is okay to take risks and to fail?
- Does my child understand that there is growth in failure?
- Has my child learned that they are perfectly okay exactly as they are in this moment?

The ultimate goal of mindful parenting is emotional freedom. Such liberation is found within oneself as it is entirely independent of material possessions or conventional notions of success, and it is the greatest wealth one can acquire. For a mindful parent, freedom lies in the knowledge that their child's life cannot and should not be controlled. That parent knows that life will come at their child, and that their child has developed the skills to engage with it, tolerate it, and ultimately prevail.

A child who is parented mindfully knows that they are loved unconditionally, not for their achievements but for who they are in all their passion and rawness. This child experiences freedom as they can trust that the universe is abundant and will provide.

Ultimately, true freedom requires surrender to all that parents and their children may experience in all its muck, glory, and pain. Most parents live under the illusion of freedom, but sadly only those who are actually conscious souls have learned the truth about untethering from conditioned thoughts and habits.

Freedom is a deep understanding that pain is not to be feared or avoided but is to be experienced. There is no suffering for those who comprehend these lessons. **Life's real lessons are learned in the mess of it all.**

The greatest joys in life stem from the priceless relationship parents create with their children when they bond through connection rather than through using correction and control, while gently asserting essential boundaries to contain and guide their children. Through conscious parenting, this sacred relationship between parent and child can provide the greatest path to freedom and authenticity. **A mindful parent fully understands that their children are not theirs to hold on to tightly, but their own beings who need to fly freely, always remembering that what their children believe about themselves is what they will become.**

NOTES

PART 4
THE CONSCIOUS TOOLBOX

The aim of the earlier sections of this book has been to introduce you to a different approach to parenting where you cede control, manage your ego, and recognize your child's inherent worth. This is a challenging process as you reorient yourself to a new way of thinking, being, and interacting with your children.

I have created this Conscious Toolbox to give you practical tools to implement these lessons. They are intended as guides and can be used individually or collectively. Trust yourself to figure out exactly what your child needs in each moment and select from these pragmatic tools to support your efforts. Mindful parenting is not a linear path. Inevitably, there will be steps forward and setbacks, all of which are to be embraced with neutrality and self-love.

Role Play

Role play is an effective tool to teach a child how to handle either a situation that might be complex for their age or an emotion that might be difficult for them to manage in a given situation. Engaging in role play can teach a child to comprehend a battery of emotions. It can also develop empathy in a child.

As the child plays the role of each person involved in a given situation, they actually get to experience that person's experience. This technique gives the child a chance to embody the role of each person involved in a dispute so that they can understand first-hand the feelings of each participant. This in turn teaches them how to manage both their behavior and their emotions.

Hands Off

When eight-year-old Jordan got excited at school and craved attention, he became physical toward his classmates and was frequently being admonished and punished by his teachers. He explained to his parents that when he became agitated and frustrated, he acted out aggressively to try to get attention. He found it hard to control his behavior. In role-playing this scenario, his father pretended to be Jordan as he elbowed his wife, who also pretended to be a girl standing in line next to him. The wife yelled at the father and said she did not want to be his friend anymore.

After this simple interaction, the family deconstructed how it felt to all of them and asked Jordan what he observed. The goal was to teach him to have empathy for the kid he elbowed. He was asked how he would feel if a classmate did this to him. Then the family role played that scenario in different ways.

First, Jordan pretended to be the kid who was pushed by Jordan. When he was ready, he was allowed to be himself while his parents tried to trigger the feeling in him that made him become aggressive. In that moment, they yelled "freeze" and discussed both their emotions, and whether there are other techniques he could use to self-soothe without resorting to physicality. Jordan realized that when he was feeling triggered and upset and was about to act out, instead he could walk away, go to the bathroom, take a drink of water, write his feelings on a Post-It to show his parents later, or simply take a deep breath.

The three family members discussed these strategies which helped him to feel calmer. He also found that a deep breath gave him a chance to think before he acted. Jordan then wrote these strategies on a list to take with him to school.

His parents also reminded him that the feelings that arise within him, and seem so overwhelming in any given moment, are temporary and will pass in a few minutes if he simply allows them to without acting on them, while the feelings that arise in the other child who was hurt may last much longer. Jordan also liked the idea that if he just wanted to be seen by a classmate to say hello and get attention, he could create special signals such as a salute, high-five, or fun handshake.

Distraction

In lieu of criticism or correction, distraction provides an effective way to connect without drama, particularly in younger children whose language skills may not allow them to express their feelings adequately. Where a child is upset because of a physical or emotional need that has arisen, it can be helpful to distract that child with humor or with a soothing activity.

Clean Up Your Act

Three-year-old Dina loved to play in the mud with her older sister. Given a bucket, water, and dirt, she could play for hours. One day while making mud pies, she became hungry. She entered her home and asked her mother Eileen for lunch. Her mother asked her to wash her hands while she prepared her lunch which unexpectedly prompted a huge tantrum as Dina refused to wash her hands.

It was apparent to her mother, who was so attuned to her patterns, that her blood sugar had dropped and that she would be difficult to console in that moment. Naturally, she could not eat lunch with mud caked on her hands and under her fingernails.

Her mother calmly and quickly came up with an idea. She went into the playroom and retrieved Dina's favorite bag of small, plastic Disney characters. She dumped them into the bathroom sink which she filled with soapy water and asked Dina to give her favorite figurine toys a bath while she prepared lunch. This idea was enticing to Dina who promptly went to the sink and meticulously washed her toys. She even called out to her mother for more soap! Shortly thereafter, lunch was served to the child with the cleanest hands around without any argument. Crisis and disconnection were averted as all needs were met.

Nurture Nature

During times of great hardship and emotional turmoil, it is wise to seek out natural beauty both for the calmness it inspires and the lessons it teaches. Nature is the best reminder that everything in life is temporary, including the hard times that each one of us experiences. Just by watching the clouds shift and noticing the leaves change, we are reminded that nothing in life is permanent.

Nature also reminds us that we are small in the vast complexity of the world, yet we matter infinitely. Just as each leaf or snowflake is unique and has a role to play in the world's ecosystem, so true is it that the world would not be the same without the presence of each human soul with their unique gifts. Nature can provide a calming influence in our lives.

Offer Options

Another simple yet effective tool for dealing with children of all ages is to offer two or three options in any given situation. The options should be based on the child's age, ability, judgment, and stage of development.

Once choices are presented, the parent should honor the choice the child or teenager accepted. In advance, the parent should be sure that all of the options offered are reasonable and tenable, and that rejecting any of them is also a valid decision on the child's part. Offering more than a few choices becomes confusing and should be avoided.

Offering options teaches children decision-making. Often children get confused when asked to make even the simplest decision, such as vanilla or chocolate. The parent should refrain from offering input or advice, and simply allow the child to choose, explaining that any choice is a good choice and that if the child is unhappy with their choice, they can make a change.

While this seems like an easy tool that promotes mindful connection, parents often find that they seek to control their child's choices and they get upset if their child disagrees with them. Even the youngest of children should be given choices. Allow the child to wear stripes with polka dots if they choose.

The less the parent seeks to control a child's choices, provided that they are safe, the less likely it is that the child will be angry and rebellious during the adolescent years. Providing and honoring choices informs a child that they are being heard and that their opinion is valid and matters.

Where a child repeatedly finds it hard to choose among several options, they are probably feeling insecure and have not learned to trust their own judgment. They should be taught to tune in to their intuition. Their gut instinct is an excellent, albeit often overlooked tool. Both parents and children would be well-served to reacquaint themselves with their inner knowing and to follow their instincts. They can do so by remembering an important strategy: **Don't think about it, feel about it!**

Autonomy Rocks

Later that day, after Dina finished her lunch, Eileen was babysitting for her beloved five-year-old neighbor, Maya. The plan was for them to walk together to the neighborhood pool to meet Maya's friends for a day of swimming. Before leaving, Maya was playing with Dina. The girls were scavenging in the yard and they happily discovered handfuls of rocks and stones which they admired.

It was finally time to walk to the pool. Since there are no sidewalks in their neighborhood, Maya was told that she would have to leave some of her rocks at home so that Eileen could hold her hand while they walked to the pool. Eileen explained that since Maya is small, cars might not see her. Maya refused to give up any of her precious rocks to hold Eileen's hand and instead she went into a tantrum. She wanted to take every rock in her collection to the pool to show her friends. Since they filled both hands, she refused to hold Eileen's hand.

Eileen decided to offer Maya several options. She could place the rocks in a bag to take to the pool so that she would have one free hand; she could leave them behind and retrieve them later; or they could skip the pool playdate and stay back and play.

Maya calmed down and asked Eileen for a bag in which to carry her rocks. Ironically, later that day Maya never bothered playing with her rock collection at the pool and never showed them to her friends. At the end of the day, Eileen asked her if she wanted to keep her precious bag of stones and she declined.

It was apparent to Eileen that Maya was more concerned with having agency over her choices than actually playing with the bag of rocks. Once she was given choices, and the option she selected was honored, her need for control dissipated.

Generally, the content of a dispute with a child is less important than the feelings that the dispute triggers. When the underlying emotional or physical need is met, such as the need for agency and control in this situation, often the issue and related tension resolves.

A Chilly Lesson

> *Fourteen-year-old Mike refused to take his new sweater to school. While the family lives in Florida, his mother Melanie insisted that he wear it as the school is air-conditioned. This disagreement devolved into a huge*

fight between mother and son, and Mike stormed off to school without his sweater. He preferred to walk than to let his mother drive him.

As she did not want a repeat of this scenario, Melanie decided that a different strategy was in order the next day. After considering the situation, she realized that she was more upset that Mike generally refused to listen to her and follow her instructions, than about his refusal to take a sweater to school. This dispute had little to do with the sweater and more to do with the way her son was speaking to her.

Melanie decided that instead of demanding that Mike wear his new sweater to school the next morning, she would offer him several options. He could wear his old hoodie; wear the new sweater; take the new sweater to school and leave it in his locker in case he got cold; or go without a sweater entirely.

He opted not to take a sweater. If he got cold at school, he would be uncomfortable, and that consequence would be enough of a lesson. The discord between parent and son dissipated when Melanie realized that she cannot and need not control and micromanage all of Mike's decisions.

> *The options which Melanie offered Mike removed the element of control which she had attempted to exert over him. Also, Mike was old enough to make wardrobe decisions on his own and was well aware that he would have to abide by the consequences of his choices.*

Even a child as young as five could have been offered these same choices and their decision should be honored. A parent should not and need not shield their child from the consequences of their decisions unless their safety is at risk or the incident involves an important family value.

Creative solutions such as distraction and options can often avoid drama and arguments which inherently wound a child who may feel that they have no agency over their decisions. This requires the parent to let go of the need to exert control over everything that happens to their child. With some flexibility and resourcefulness, parents can develop alternatives in the moment that can help make their children feel heard and feel sovereign.

Turn Criticism to Compliments

It is easy to become frustrated and triggered by a child. Parents can literally go from feeling calm to feeling infuriated without skipping a beat. This is why it is critical for parents to use the tools of mindfulness, including the pause and the breath, before expressing their agitation. Every time a child is yelled at, whether for a minor or more significant infraction, the child's spirit is wounded.

When a child is challenging a parent, it is wise for the parent to consider mindful and neutral ways to respond which do not involve criticism or anger. Consider these alternative ways of responding: "It is great that you pushed every button on the elevator panel, now we get to stop at every floor!" or "I love the way you want to be independent and cross the street alone. Soon you will be tall enough to do that." These types of responses work particularly well with younger children.

Parents often challenge this concept as it relates to older children who have breached essential boundaries and are engaging in dangerous behaviors. However, under such circumstances, the conscious parenting paradigm is even more important.

It is critical for the parent to find something about which to compliment the teenager at that moment, rather than to criticize or correct them. For example, a parent can say, "I am so grateful that you texted me at 3:00 a.m. for a ride home rather than taking a ride from an intoxicated friend." This is not to say that the issue of underage and excessive drinking need not be addressed, but merely that you are acknowledging that your child made a wise choice under trying circumstances. When the teen sobers up, then the parent can address the needs beneath the teen's behavior and try to create strategies for better decision-making and choices in the future.

Avoid Labels

Ironically, the parent who labels their child based on the child's behavior tends to create the undesirable behavior that they seek to avoid. For example, the child who is chronically called "lazy" tends to become a lazy student. Labeling a child can cause that child to associate themselves with that very label which, for obvious reasons, does not serve the child.

If a child is exhibiting a behavior that is less than desirable, the parent would be well-served to help them work towards finding new modes of behavior in mindful ways, while avoiding labels, negative comments, or judgments about the existing behavior.

Rather than labeling a child negatively, the parent would be well served to realize that the undesirable behavior often represents an unmet emotional need or possibly an organic issue. It is wise for the parent to work to figure out what that need or issue is, and then take steps to meet or treat it. This will provide a more longstanding solution to the problem while the child will not associate themselves with that behavior.

Where parents have children tested and diagnosed in order for the child to get extra test time or other services, it is important for the parent to try not to continuously associate the child with their particular diagnosis to the extent possible and where the healthcare provider agrees. **Where the child is persistently labeled based on their diagnosis, the child may either feel stigmatized and permanently damaged, or they may rely on it as an excuse for not trying as hard to overcome obstacles.** Even where a child has organic issues and disabilities, mindful parenting offers the tools to create self-esteem through acceptance, connection, and boundaries.

Set the Conditions

The parents' behavior, tone, body language, and energy, as well as physical space and household rules, help to set the conditions for their children's behavior. Parents literally set the stage for their children's actions both within and outside of the home. For example, where children are easily distracted during homework time, the parents should create a quiet, clutter-free, clean space for homework that is free of devices and well stocked with school supplies.

Parents are the role model for the behavior they seek to support in their children. If they have their own work to do at night, they could sit with their child and quietly focus on it or assist their child with homework. Parents often say to their children, "Do as I say, not as I do" however this simply does not work, although as a parent I can surely understand the temptation to try to enforce this mindless notion.

Parents who want their children to shut off their devices by a set time at night must do the same with their own devices. The often-heard retort by the parent that they need their phone or iPad for work does not send the right message. For children, Snapchatting and playing video games with friends is their work, and they are not going to stop when their parents refuse to follow suit. Similarly, if parents want to limit the intake of sweets, parents must limit their own dessert intake. The same rings true for exercise and musical instrument practice.

Parents are the role models for their children's emotional tolerance, physical well-being, and spiritual practices. The adage by which parents should live is, "**Do as I do!**"

Get Buy-In

As stated earlier, when parents want to set rules around essential boundaries, there is a much greater chance that their children, particularly their older children, will follow those rules when they are engaged in the process of setting them. **Where a child has participated in setting household rules about behavior, they have a feeling of buy-in and are more likely to follow those rules.**

Household rules should primarily concern issues surrounding safety and values. This is particularly true when dealing with teenagers. Rules should not be set merely because a parent finds themselves upset when their child is out of sight or because the parent does not like the child's choice of friends.

Parents and children should sit together to discuss expectations such as homework, chores, curfew, socializing, and driving privileges. Each child's needs and preferences should be considered and addressed. When parents refuse to accede to their child's wishes, they need to provide a cogent reason that is free from the desire for control. Similarly, inculcating fear in a child is a mindless approach as it merely creates anxiety without producing behavioral changes.

If necessary, parents can actually create a contract with their children so that rules are set in writing and everyone has ample notice of expectations. A cell phone contract that clearly delineates privileges and boundaries can be signed by everyone in the family. It should incorporate remedies and consequences for those situations when the limits and boundaries are trespassed. A cell phone contract may include some of the following terms:

- The child is expected to answer the call of a parent promptly or text as soon as possible.

- The parent will activate software that allows the parent to locate their child at all times which will not be turned off.
- The phone will be charged at all times, and the child will carry a charger.
- The child will turn over their phone at any time for the parent to see what the child is doing or viewing.
- The parent will not secretly look at the child's phone.
- The child will give the parent all of their passwords.
- The child agrees not to use their or their friends' phones to view materials that would be objectionable to the parents.
- The child will not send texts or emails, or say anything on the phone, that they would not otherwise be willing to express to someone in person.
- The child agrees not to use the phone for any inappropriate behavior such as sexting or bullying.
- The child agrees to turn off their phone at 10:00 p.m. (or another agreed-upon time) and will keep it off until the following morning.
- All family members agree not to use phones or devices during family meals.

√

Mediation and Reflection

Mediation is a form of alternative dispute resolution in the legal world. It is also an effective tool that can be used in any group dynamic, including a family, to assist in resolving disputes. Mediation helps family members identify issues, get unstuck, communicate effectively, listen carefully, dissolve power struggles, and facilitate deeper connection.

If there is a family member who is not directly involved in a particular dispute, that person can agree to act as the mediator. Also, each family member can take turns leading a mediation. The mediator must agree to be neutral and not take sides. The mediator can make and enforce simple rules that might include:

- Everyone must speak respectfully in calm tones.
- Everyone must be honest, and all relevant facts must be stated. Omitting important facts is not honest.
- Everyone must turn off their devices and focus on the process, even those family members who are not directly involved in the dispute.
- No one will embarrass anyone else.
- Everyone must agree not to share anything that occurs during the mediation, or any information about the problem, outside of the family.

Reflection is a tool that can be used in the process of mediation to help people hear one another in a new way. Reflection involves having the mediator listen to each person without interruption and then restate what that person said. The mediator should continue to express what the participant said until the speaker confirms that the mediator got it right and was heard properly. Then the other person should get the same opportunity to speak, and the mediator should reflect back what was said. This should continue until everyone has been heard. Then the parties can be asked to repeat what the other person said.

Since mediation is a process which is to be controlled by the parties, the mediator is there only to act as a conduit to help everyone communicate more effectively. Each family member can suggest solutions or compromises, but no one can be forced to accept them. Ultimately, the goal of mediation involves effectuating communication rather than reaching solutions. If solutions are reached, that is great but if not, the parties can agree to disagree unless safety or family values are at risk.

Sibling Rivalry

One essential element of handling sibling rivalry is remembering that the parent should never take sides. The parent's role in the dispute is not to mete out justice or get to the "right" answer. Rather, it is to help the children navigate the dispute on their own and learn to compromise. Often sibling disputes are intended to get the parents' attention. The siblings are not usually fighting over the thing about which they appear to be fighting. Instead, they are trying to be seen and heard.

When the parent intervenes in an attempt to be the fact-finder and to resolve the dispute or reach a compromise, the children often get stuck in their respective positions. This is why the content of the argument never really matters. Instead, the parents' goal should be to hear each child, reflect back their respective grievances, find commonalities, create physical space between the children when necessary, and honor each child's position.

When the parent serves as the neutral mediator rather than the arbiter of the facts, the children feel heard. It is important that the parent avoids taking sides and favoring one child over the other as this inevitably creates more discord.

Parents should resist the temptation to do any of the following:

- Find fault in either or both children.
- Adjudicate the dispute.
- Attach labels to either or both children.
- Take sides.
- Determine a winner and a loser.
- Compare the children to one another.

A mindful parent should:

- Allow each child to be heard.
- Reflect each child's feelings and position.
- Assist each child in using language that helps them communicate their position and feelings.
- Observe the role that each child is playing to ascertain if there is a pattern.
- Discern the dynamic that has evolved between the children.
- Encourage each child to reflect and ventilate about what happened and how they are feeling.
- Uphold family boundaries and values.
- Separate the children from one another where the dispute has become physical for cooling off.
- Identify new ways to help them communicate more effectively.
- Identify possible solutions.
- Remain calm and neutral.
- Solicit suggestions from each child about how to reach a compromise.

Special Time

The use of special time is a powerful tool to allow each parent to connect with each child in the family individually on a regular basis. It involves allocating a specific amount of time for each parent and child to do something special alone together at regular intervals as their respective schedules permit. The child should have as much control and say as possible in determining how they would like to spend their special time with each of their parents individually, although the parent can set the amount of time and the schedule. It is best if this is done one-on-one with each parent and child.

If a child chooses to play catch with their dad or kick a soccer ball with their mom, then this constitutes the activity for special time. The activity can be as simple as taking a walk or reading a book aloud together. It is advisable to avoid using this time to view things on devices, and both parent and child can agree to this in advance.

Activities that do not involve devices are preferable, as is playing with toys that are neither electronic nor battery powered. Toys that require the input of energy from the user usually involve more creativity.

The child will know that on a particular day of the week for a specified amount of time, they will have their parent's undivided attention. Both parent and child can look forward to this sacred space for them to connect. It is a powerful tool to express to that child just how important they are in their parent's life. It creates special memories.

During special time, which can affectionately be called "ST," the parent should avoid attending to anyone or anything other than that child. If the phone or doorbell rings, it is important for the parent to inform their caller or visitor that they cannot speak at the moment because they are enjoying special time with their child. It is empowering and joyful for a child to hear their parent tell another adult that their time with their child is so important that another adult may not interrupt it.

Since it can be hard to end ST, it is wise for the parent to set a timer for the specified amount of time so that the child knows that when the timer rings, ST has to end. Doing so will avoid the parent having to be the "bad guy" by ending ST. The parent can express their own disappointment when ST is over for the night. With younger children, the end of the stated ST interval may still cause the child to tantrum, but the parent can handle it with mindfulness allowing the full expression of that child's disappointment while maintaining that boundary.

Family Meetings

Unlike ST, family meetings at regular intervals allow the entire family to connect as a unit. They are intended to allow each family member to express feelings about their week and about how things are going within the family and in their respective lives.

Each family member should be given the chance to lead the meeting and set the agenda, which of course should be age-appropriate. Also, during these meetings, each family member should be given an opportunity to speak without interruption. A special stuffed toy or cherished item may be selected by the leader to be used so that everyone knows that the person holding the item cannot be interrupted.

Any subject can be raised by a family member during the family meeting without fear of admonishment or retribution. This provides an opportunity for each child to express their feelings, address disputes that may have arisen during the week with siblings or parents, complain, or show gratitude. Whatever issue each person raises should not be criticized.

Instead, the family can work together to brainstorm and create solutions where necessary. The leader can be creative in deciding where in the house the meeting should be held, and snacks can be provided. The leader should be given free rein to make the family meeting they are running special.

The point of family meetings is to let each family member know that their voice matters in the collective unit and will be heard. It also allows family members to learn to negotiate and to compromise. It is yet another powerful vehicle for teaching leadership, effective listening, and cooperation.

When necessary, mediation can be used during a family meeting when disputes arise although the purpose of most family meetings should be collective connection. Family meetings can also be used to plan family outings, vacations, or birthday celebrations, to navigate challenges that a family member may be experiencing, or to set rules concerning daily chores and homework.

Teachable Moments: Listening Without Lecturing

Do not lecture, just listen. This suggestion cannot be stressed strongly enough. As tempting as it is to lecture children of all ages, it is counterproductive. Any parent who recalls their own childhood is likely to remember how much lectures were both disliked and disregarded.

Rather than speaking, silence by a parent sets the conditions for open discussion. The child will feel heard and will be more willing to talk where the parent can contain their anxiety and allow the full expression of their child's emotions and concerns. This is how the parent can be the container for those emotions and hold space, as well as how the child will learn to process and tolerate all of their emotions.

When a parent is deeply attuned to their child, they will seize teachable moments as they arise. An attuned parent will be aware when the child is open to learning a lesson. For example, when a young child seated in a car observes the driver of an adjacent car smoking a cigarette, the child may inquire about it.

A child's questions present the perfect moment for the parent to provide facts that teach their children about important subjects without lecturing or judging. Such moments offer opportunities to introduce new ideas such as cigarette addiction on an age-appropriate level. It is important for parents to seize every opportunity to teach lessons and raise important safety issues while refraining from lectures wherever possible.

As time goes on, subjects will come up repeatedly and can be discussed again, each time with more information and answers. The parent and child can do online research about a topic, although where possible the parent should do the research in advance and gently direct the child to age-appropriate articles or websites.

The key is to allow the child to drive the conversation. The parent's goal should be to usher the child toward the relevant and truthful facts, while entertaining all associated feelings that arise. A child who knows that they can have a discussion with their parent without being lectured or judged will feel more comfortable to go to their parent when things are troubling them. This approach offers yet another vehicle towards increased connection.

Use Direct-Examination, not Cross-Examination

Children do not like to be peppered with questions. While it is tempting to parents to want all the details about their children's lives, whether about their school day, a playdate, or a party they attended, the parent would be wise to check their own desire for information and to recognize that it is the child's right to decide whether to talk or to withhold information.

Whether a child is more willing to share details of their lives with their parents will depend in large measure on the way that the parent approaches these conversations. While the child's temperament also plays a role, the parent can either support or quash the degree to which their child discloses information about events and feelings based on whether their approach is conscious or unconscious.

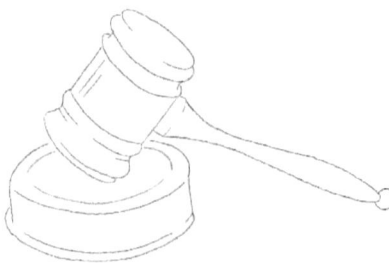

In the mindful approach, it is important for parents to discern their child's readiness to share their experiences, and also the energy they bring when approaching the conversation. Are they neutral about it or do they have a searing need to know which stems from their own fears?

One useful tool in containing a parent's fear and anxiety is to ask the child open-ended questions. In the law, this is referred to as "direct-examination" and it is used to question a friendly witness at a legal proceeding, one who is on their side. The purpose is to allow the person who is testifying to tell their story without suggesting any answers. This is a great approach with children.

On the other hand, "cross-examination" involves pointed, specific questions which suggest the answer. It is allowed at a legal proceeding when a witness is considered hostile to their side. These questions often require the person to give only a "yes" or "no" answer with little or no explanation, as the answer is suggested within the question.

Since children are not akin to hostile, unfriendly witnesses in legal matters, a parent should be mindful to use the direct-examination approach when engaging their children in conversation, and then to be prepared to hear whatever the child has on their mind. The child who learns that their parent can tolerate whatever the child reports is more likely to be open and to share more details.

For example, a parent should consider asking their child how their school day was, rather than asking if they had a nice day. This seemingly innocuous difference actually sends a message to the child that either the parent is willing to hear whatever the child has to say without regard to whether it is "positive" or "negative," or whether the parent only wants to hear that their day was "good" or "nice." Once the parent decides to ask a question in this manner, then they should try not to interrupt their child and allow the story to unfold. Often, bedtime provides the best atmosphere for more open communication as the child has had time to process the events of their day, and they are less guarded.

Honesty is the Best Policy

Connection promotes honest discussion of all subjects at appropriate age levels and developmental stages. If the parent speaks openly and accurately on any subject about which their child is inquisitive, the child will learn from that parent not only about behavioral expectations but also about the inherent risks of a specific behavior.

Speak openly without fear and anxiety. Stop giving information when the child's questions stop. A child will only ask questions to the extent that they are ready for the answers, so the parent should remain attuned and discern their child's needs and willingness to learn in that moment.

A parent who lies to their child, even about small things, creates distrust which fosters disconnection. This is not intended to suggest that children need to know things in the family that do not concern them, that are beyond their emotional level of understanding, or about which they have no control. However, once a parent decides to discuss a topic with their child and to answer their questions, honesty should prevail even on difficult subjects.

For example, when a child hears about a death and asks the parent whether either they or that parent will die, it is unwise to say "no" as this is false. When the child learns that the parent was not truthful, that child may no longer trust information that they provide. Even with less important matters, lying breaks the bond of trust and connection.

As a corollary matter, parents should not use fear to try to control their child's behavior. Fear is as wounding as reactivity and does not serve to create a bond of trust or a sense of safety. For example, when a toddler is having a tantrum in a store, it is unwise for the parent to threaten to leave that child alone in the store unless they stop screaming, as the parent has no intention of doing so. While it may accomplish the immediate goal of stopping the tantrum, the long-term impact of the threat of being abandoned is damaging to the child's sense of well-being and safety.

Alternatively, where the parent's efforts to support the child and help them process their tantrum fail, the parent can inform the child that if they cannot calm down soon, they will all have to leave the store (or the party), and then the parent should follow through while remaining calm but clear. This is yet another way of enforcing a healthy boundary around untoward behavior without inculcating fear and distrust through lying.

As always, the child's underlying unmet need beneath the behavior which prompted the tantrum should be investigated and met. Similarly, with older children and teenagers, fear should not be used as a mechanism for control. Rather, connection and boundaries should always prevail as mindful tools.

Powerful Phrases

- I love you no matter what.
- I hear you.

- Tell me more.
- You are so strong.
- How are you feeling?
- Everything is temporary.
- This is not the whole story.
- It is okay to feel angry, sad, or jealous.
- I see your point.
- Can you see this from their point of view?
- You got this.
- Take a deep breath.
- I'm already proud of you.
- I believe in you.
- I trust you.
- Can I help?
- It's okay; it happens.

Say This Instead of That

While parents intend to help and support their children, they often either assert too much pressure on their children or are more negative than they realize. Here are some examples of how messages can be delivered more mindfully.

Rather than saying...	Instead say...
"Stop being so negative!"	"I understand why you're feeling that way."
"Never give up."	"You've tried really hard, and sometimes it's okay to stop."
"You are a bad child."	"I am disappointed in your behavior."
"Stop crying!"	"I can see you are upset. What's troubling you?"
"You're wrong!"	"I see your point of view."
"Hurry up! You're NEVER ready on time."	"We have to leave in ten minutes."
"How many times do I have to explain this?"	"I'll explain it again. Let's try it together."
"You're doing it wrong!"	"Can I show you another way to try it"?
"Stop complaining and whining!"	"I see you're upset about this."
"What a mess you made!"	"Looks like you had fun. Can I help you clean it up?"
"It's not that hard."	"I know it's hard, but I have confidence you can do it."
"I will not tolerate that tone/language!"	"Something must be bothering you. Let's talk about it."
"You may not speak to me like that!"	"Please use kinder words and a softer voice. I'm willing to listen."

Promote Opportunities for Service

Parents who teach children the importance of service to others inculcate important values including empathy and gratitude. Teaching about service can begin early in life. It creates self-esteem, self-confidence, and a sense of belonging to the greater community.

Families who volunteer in activities together teach their children that everyone has a role and responsibility in protecting their community and supporting others. This in turn helps children learn empathy, humility, and gratitude. As children age, they should be expected to do volunteer work which interests them as they should have a voice in choosing the organizations and activities for which to volunteer.

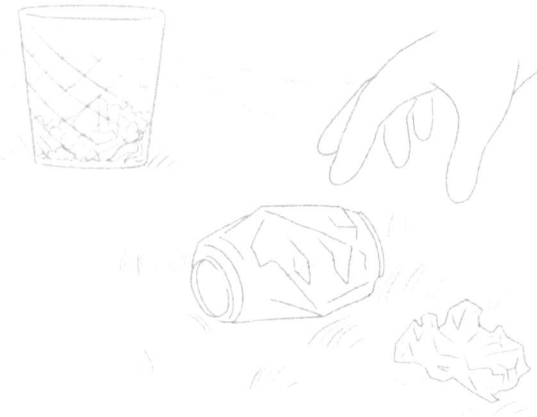

Feeling involved and knowing that you have made a difference in the life of another person can feel empowering and gratifying. It also offers children a sense of purpose and belonging, and can expose them to new activities and interests.

Service is as important to the person who is serving as it is to the person who is being helped. It offers a sense of gratification and self-satisfaction. When parents complain that their children lack gratitude, finding opportunities for their children to serve others is the first place they should turn.

Promote Opportunities for Self-Expression

There are many ways for children to feel heard and worthy. As you have learned, you help your children to feel valued by listening deeply, asserting necessary boundaries, and withholding shame, judgment, and criticism.

Another way to help your children find their voices is to provide opportunities for them to express their opinions. Encourage them to speak up in an authentic, yet respectful manner when something is troubling them, and they want to effect change. Doing so allows children to understand that not only do they have a voice in the world, but they have a chance to implement change even in small ways.

Here is a great example of how a terrific 3rd-grader, Olivia, chose to express her gratitude. Her purpose was to let the store know that the change it implemented was meaningful to her and should continue. Olivia felt empowered writing this letter. Think about ways in which you could empower your children to let their voices be heard.

> Dear Old navy,
>
> Thank you for labeling clothes unizex in the store. I am a 9 year old girl 3rd grade.
>
> I have a sporty style and like athletic clothes. I have never liked wearing glitter rainbows and unicorns. That is all they have in the girls aisle so I usually shop in the Boys aisle. It bothered me to shop there.
>
> I always thought clothes should be for eauryon I wish more stores would do what you have done. I will always shop at old navy because I can proudly shop in those ailse.
>
> Sincerely,
> Olivia

Practice Self-Care, Meditation, and Self-Compassion

Self-care is not selfish. A parent who is overwhelmed, exhausted, and stressed cannot mindfully parent their children. While parents often complain that they do not have the time to care for themselves, it is essential that they find even the smallest amount of time to look inward and feed their own souls. Sleep, exercise, and proper nutrition are not luxuries, nor are grown-up social outlets and activities of interest. Rather, they are essential to the parents' own well-being. Also, where parents practice self-care, they are providing effective role models to their children for a life well-lived.

Since parenting is all about the parent as this book illustrates, it stands to reason that an adult must raise themselves first in order to be effective parents. This includes the importance of remaining calm and feeling joyful. It requires focus on the parents' emotional, physical, social, and spiritual life. Just as in airplanes where passengers are instructed to put on their own oxygen masks first, parents must take care of their needs first in order to effectively care for their children.

Meditation is an essential tool to parenting mindfully and living consciously. It teaches people that their thoughts are not real as they are merely constructs of longstanding patterns. Therefore, meditation is a vehicle that teaches detachment from longstanding patterns of thought which in turn can create the space and open-mindedness for shifts in perspectives.

Meditation also has a calming influence and can be done in any given moment merely by focusing on your breath. During that moment when a person is focused on their breath, they are not focused on other extraneous thoughts. In this way, meditation can reduce anxiety and promote self-awareness. Even young children can learn to meditate and can appreciate its benefits.

Self-compassion is another essential element of self-care. Many parents who awaken from an earlier model of parenting which was less mindful and was based on what they learned as children, often feel distraught that they did not learn the skills of mindful parenting earlier in their children's lives. They worry that they have damaged their children, but it is important to remember that it is never too late to learn these new skills and that this is the only moment they have.

To focus on past regrets inherently means that the focus is on the past which is already gone. Similarly, worrying is focused on the future which has not yet arrived. Therefore, the only moment that we have is now, and this is the moment that matters. **Attend to this moment with self-compassion and consciousness, as this moment co-creates the next moment and this is our greatest superpower.**

Mindful parenting cannot be practiced without self-care and self-compassion with the understanding that each parent is doing their best in each moment based on their present state of awareness. The work of every parent is to raise their awareness with compassion and understanding while remaining flexible, curious, and open to change.

Keep a Journal

A journal is a wonderful tool to promote mindfulness. The very act of writing about thoughts and feelings helps to separate from them. Most people repeat the same thoughts and get stuck in unconscious patterns of thoughts which lead to immutable outcomes. Parents need to reparent themselves so that in turn, they can parent their children more mindfully without repeating old patterns and passing them on to the next generation.

Journaling is also a great vehicle for self-expression. There are no rules or requirements when keeping a journal. Rather, the writer need only allow the free flow of thoughts, ideas, and feelings. Keeping a journal affords a private space for the unhindered and untainted expression of the self.

It also affords the parent the opportunity to manage and assess growth over time. The very nature of the written word helps to organize thoughts, to record feelings, to monitor progress, and ultimately to separate from and release longstanding thought patterns and habits over time.

Journaling is a great tool for children as well, the youngest of whom can keep a diary of pictures and over time can progress to writing as they grow and develop new skills. It promotes self-reflection, self-awareness, and creativity.

Inculcate Gratitude

Gratitude is a wonderful vehicle for a joyful life, and it supports the manifestation of one's deepest desires. A parent who complains incessantly and feels victimized is likely to raise a child who is a complainer and a victim. Conversely, a parent who routinely appreciates and expresses the bounty in their life is likely to raise a child who does the same.

Parents often wonder why their child is ungrateful without realizing their role in co-creating this unhealthy paradigm. A child who is demanding and unappreciative probably has had few limits imposed upon them involving either material things or behaviors. Remembering the adage that "less is more" as it will go a long way in instilling a sense of gratitude in a child.

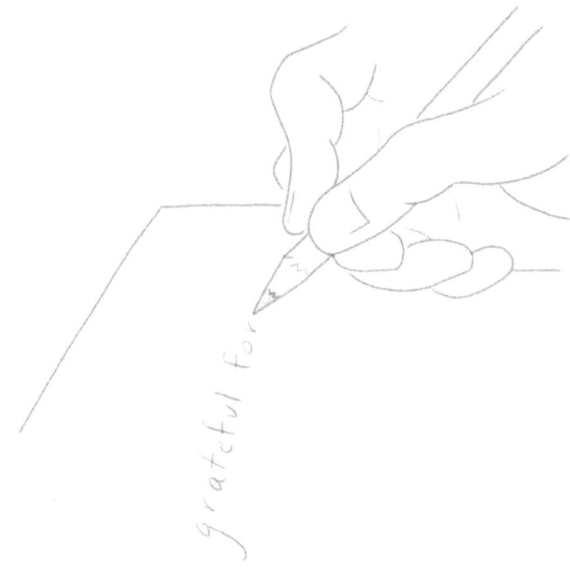

The child who is given too much without adequate boundaries and limits tends to have expectations that become hard to meet. This is the child who is likely to become demanding and cannot easily be satisfied. Also, the parent is the best role model for a life of gratitude. Where the parent expresses their thanks to people they encounter and for the things they have, the child learns to do the same.

A gratitude practice can be implemented in routines from bedtime to family meetings. Also, a gratitude journal is a wonderful way to teach a child to recognize and express thanks regularly. Where the parents express their gratitude for the small and large gifts in their lives, their children learn to do the same. **The energy of gratitude, rather than that of victimhood, incessant craving, and lack of appreciation, increases self-worth and happiness.**

THE CONSCIOUS TOOLBOX   233

Send Your Child a Note to Thank Them for Raising You

Every day provides a new opportunity for a parent to express love and gratitude to their child. Milestones moments serve as a great reminder that our children are here to teach and guide us towards our highest self. Small moments also offer that chance. A simple note in a lunchbox is yet another opportunity for connection even when the parent and child are physically separated.

I hold my daughters in the highest regard and have deep and infinite gratitude, love, and admiration for the young women they have become and for the remarkable gifts that they have bestowed on me. My connection with my children is my greatest blessing. Mother's Day is one of many perfect opportunities to express these sentiments. Perhaps I will even make them breakfast in bed!

One recent Mother's Day, I sent this letter to my daughters:

Dear Deena and Sara,

It feels most appropriate to wish you both a Happy Mother's Day because you are the ones who birthed me! I became a mother thanks to both of you and this was my deepest desire. Being your mother has been my greatest gift and most sacred blessing. In your own special ways, each of you has been the most incredible source of joy, inspiration, and growth for me. You are my greatest teachers.

I want you both to know that you mean more to me than any vacation, jewels, or other material items ever could. You are the roof above my head and the ground beneath my feet as you are my home. Thank you for inviting me into your lives, for caring so much, and for sharing yourselves with me. I am most honored and humbled to walk this path with you as your mother.

Each of you is finding your unique, authentic, and distinct voice yet you share the most important values - kindness, loyalty, empathy, honesty, caring, discipline, gentleness, generosity, and love. I only hope that I can be your best Producer, as you are each the greatest Director of your own lives. It is my pleasure to watch your lives unfold.

Please, never dim your lights or play small. Each of you has too much to offer and the world needs you.

Wherever life takes you, always know that you are loved and cherished more than words can express, but since I only have words, I am doing my best to use them here. Thank you for being you and for being mine.

Happy Mother's Day!

All my Love, MOM

NOTES

FINAL THOUGHTS

Mindful parenting is not for the faint of heart. It is a paradigm that requires time, focus, patience, practice, discipline, and lasting commitment. As parents learn to look within themselves, accept responsibility for their actions, identify and shift longstanding entrenched patterns, release their agendas, and engage more mindful parenting strategies, it is remarkable to witness life-affirming transformations in their children. Instead of clipping their children's wings, they will teach them to soar in their own special way.

These shifts in turn lead to meaningful and authentic connections between parents and their children that last a lifetime. It is deeply gratifying to parents when their children seek their advice, enjoy their company, and handle life's complexities and challenges with courage and resilience, while setting their own agendas and following their own dreams.

Parenting is a sacred task. When practiced wisely and consciously, the benefits are immeasurable. *Connection* and *boundaries* are the pivotal tenets of this work, and implementing them mindfully will build the child's inner core and strengthen the fundamental pillars on which emotional intelligence and true, lasting success are built.

As a mother, my greatest opportunities for mindful growth stem from my connection with each of my cherished daughters. It is through them that I have learned to awaken to my deeply held and conditioned patterns of egoic attachments. I continue in my ongoing quest towards greater awareness as this work is never done. I simply remain busy growing myself up!

The first crucial step is awareness of the truth that parenting is all about the parents and not about the children. Indeed, this is why it is called "parenting," not "childing." Mindfulness in parenting is the path to creating a more conscious world, one parent at a time.

And remember, success in the realm of conscious parenting is not measured by grades, wealth, achievement, social capital, status, power, or position, but by the depth of self-worth, a clear identity, inner strength, and self-esteem reflected back as humility, responsibility, resilience, respect for self, respect for others, and gratitude.

Meanwhile, do not forget to have fun along the way!

FINAL THOUGHTS 239

ACKNOWLEDGMENTS

To Dr. Shefali Tsabary, my spiritual guide, teacher, mentor, and friend, I am truly grateful for your wisdom. The lessons that I have learned from you throughout many years of friendship have provided the foundation for my personal growth and transformation, and for my work in guiding other families.

To Stephanie Larkin and the team at Red Penguin Publishers, thank you for your incredible guidance, patience, and support throughout the publishing process, and for believing in the importance of sharing this message.

To my wonderful clients, thank you for letting me into your lives in such a meaningful and intimate way, for sharing your pain and your joy, and for trusting me.

To Rachelle Varley, thank you for pushing me to dust off this manuscript and for sharing so many creative suggestions. Your friendship and encouragement are priceless. Without you, *How to Raise a Parent* would not have seen the light of day and reached the eyes of parents in need of mindful guidance.

To Rita Moser and Elayne Landau, my early readers and cherished friends, thank you for reading and editing this book, and for providing your insight, feedback, and wisdom. Your support has helped bring this book to fruition.

To my dear friends, and colleagues who have become dear friends, thank you for your love, support, and sisterhood, and for always being there for me. You know who you are, and you mean the world to me.

To David Ord, my editor, thank you for painstakingly and lovingly editing this manuscript and for encouraging me to move forward with it. I am grateful for your brilliant insights.

To Megan Mack, my illustrator, thank you for sharing your remarkable talent and creativity. Your fantastic illustrations brought my vision to life.

To my husband, Sam, thank you for decades of love and support throughout the ups and downs of our lives. Our marriage has stood the test of time and of growth, and for that, I am deeply grateful beyond what any words can express.

Finally, to my precious daughters, Deena and Sara, thank you for inviting me into your lives and allowing me to be the usher and guide in your journeys. You have given my life great meaning and my love for you is boundless. Thank you for being my greatest teachers and especially for teaching me how to raise a parent.

ABOUT THE AUTHOR

Ellen graduated from the University of Pennsylvania with a B.A. and M.A. in The History & Sociology of Science, focusing on the history of medicine. Thereafter, she earned her J.D. from The Benjamin N. Cardozo School of Law. For many years, she defended complex medical malpractice tort claims. She currently arbitrates disputes in the medical realm. She is also trained as a transformative mediator. Throughout this time, Ellen researched and studied mindful parenting and conscious living.

Ellen artfully combines her communication skills as a litigator, arbitrator, mediator, as well as certified parenting coach. After decades of learning, she founded Enlightened Parenting. Her conscious coaching skills and experience enable her clients to feel heard and understood as she teaches them to raise themselves, and in turn to elevate their children to be their truest and best selves.

www.ingramcontent.com/pod-product-compliance
Lightning Source LLC
Chambersburg PA
CBHW060352080526
44583CB00012B/280